Spark

Curriculum for Early Childhood

IMPLEMENTATION GUIDE

by Beverly S. Lewman and Susan A. Fowler

Redleaf Press

Published by: Redleaf Press
a division of Resources for Child Caring
450 N. Syndicate, Suite 5
St. Paul, MN 55104

Distributed by: Gryphon House
Mailing Address:
P.O. Box 207
Beltsville, MD 20704-0207

The contents of this curriculum and training manual were developed at the Department of Special Education in the College of Education at the University of Illinois under grant DE-H024D70012 from the U.S. Department of Education. However, those contents do not necessarily represent the policy of the Department of Education, and you should not assume endorsement by the federal government.

Material for the Child Goals chart was taken from the following sources:

L. J. Johnson, Gallagher, Cook, and Wong (1995). Critical skills for kindergarten: Perceptions from kindergarten teachers. Journal for Early Intervention.

Newborg, Stock, Wnek, Guidubaldi, and Svinicki (1984). Battelle Developmental Inventory. Allen, Texas: DLM Teaching Resources.

D. Marsden, S. Meisels, and J. Jablon (1993). The Work Sampling System, 2nd edition. Ann Arbor, Mich.: Rebus Planning Associates.

A. H. Hains, S. A. Fowler, I. Schwartz, J. E. Kottwitz, and S. E. Rosenkoetter. (1989). A comparison of preschool and kindergarten teachers' expectations for school readiness. Early Childhood Research Quarterly. 4, 75-88. Norwood, N.J.: Ablex Publishing.

Library of Congress Cataloging-in-Publication Data

Lewman, Beverly S., 1930–
    Spark curriculum for early childhood : implementation guide / by Beverly S. Lewman
and Susan A. Fowler.
        p. cm.
        Includes bibliographical references and index.
        ISBN 1-929610-10-6
        1. Early childhood education — Curricula. 2. Early childhood teachers — In-service training.
I. Fowler, Susan A. II. Title.

LB1139.4 .L49 2001
372.19—dc21

2001041734

Contents

Introduction
Overview of Spark for the Facilitator

Welcome!

This manual includes all the information you need in order to train staff to use the Spark (Skills Promoted through Arts, Reading, and Knowledge) Curriculum for Early Childhood. This introduction provides you with background information about the curriculum, a rationale for using the curriculum, information about developmentally appropriate creative arts activities, and information about ways to create an inviting environment for all children. It also contains suggestions for providing ongoing feedback to staff and ways to know when staff need refresher training.

Most of this book consists of staff training workshops. Workshops 1–4 include hands-on activities to familiarize teaching staff with Spark curricular materials and teaching strategies. Through the workshops, teachers will learn to use the creative arts as tools to teach children. Workshop 5 presents tools to help program administrators evaluate the effectiveness of the Spark curriculum in their early childhood programs. The best way to find out how well Spark is working is to observe it in the classroom, ask the parents, and ask the staff. The workshop also discusses perceptions about the curriculum, both positive and negative. Appendixes include the workshop 5 tools, plus a Child Goals chart used in several of the workshops, and a list of references.

The Purpose of the Curriculum

The Spark Curriculum for Early Childhood is a literacy-based creative arts curriculum in which young children learn developmental and school readiness skills by actively attending to stories and by participating in activities based on the arts: music and movement, visual art, and make-believe (drama). Spark is a child-centered curriculum in which children learn through hands-on, open-ended activities. The curriculum has two major educational focuses:

1. To introduce general early childhood concepts and skills through multisensory activities.

2. To enable teachers to address children's individual goals.

The curriculum may be used in inclusive classrooms to meet the learning needs of children who function at various levels. Teachers can and should adapt Spark activities to meet the needs of the children in their class.

The premise of Spark is that children learn more when they are actively engaged in activities that hold their interest. Developmentally appropriate stories, with activities centered on the arts, have the potential to be highly interesting to most young children.

The goal of Spark is to teach children developmental skills through stories, music, art, and make-believe—not to teach children to become better musicians, artists, or performers. Teachers do not need to be skilled in the arts in order to use the Spark curriculum. Rather, they should regard Spark as an opportunity to enjoy the arts with the children while they use the teaching potential inherent in good children's literature and in developmentally appropriate arts activities.

The Spark Format

The Spark curriculum takes approximately one hour a day, five days a week. Day 5 is an optional day in order to accommodate programs that operate on a four-day week and to allow for other priorities in a busy school schedule.

The curriculum includes twenty story-based weekly sets of activities. Each story and its related activities take one week to complete. The week's activities are based on a story that the teacher reads to the children every day of that week. The weekly set of activities focuses on four concepts that are drawn out of the story of the week; each concept is featured on a different day of the week. The large-group storytelling activity includes not only the reading of the story, but also a review of the previous day's activities, an interactive discussion of the story, an introduction to the concept of the day, and introductions of the center activities. Children are encouraged to be actively engaged throughout the storytelling segment.

Following the storytelling activities, the children choose a center to attend. Each center features small-group music and movement, art, or make-believe activities that reinforce the concept of the day. General early childhood goals are embedded in the activities, and teachers are encouraged to promote individual children's objectives during these small-group sessions. An adult (teacher or assistant) is present at each center, actively participating in the activity. For this reason, there can only be as many centers as there are adults in the classroom (typically the number is two, but the curriculum usually provides activities in each of the three arts areas). Children are encouraged to participate in both center activities during the Spark hour.

During the Spark story time, teachers may promote many skills, including language, memory, sequencing, cognitive, and social. As teachers introduce each activity center, they may address gross-motor, fine-motor, language, social, and problem-solving skills. When the children move into the small-group activities, teachers can promote both general and individual skills.

The Spark curriculum offers a more efficient way to organize the day because the curriculum integrates the story time and music, art, and make-believe small-group activities into one comprehensive, coordinated segment of the day.

The following chart compares a typical preschool teaching schedule, and a schedule incorporating the Spark curriculum.

Typical Schedule	Spark Schedule
8:15 Arrival/Play	8:15 Arrival/Play
9:15 Story	8:30 Spark Time
9:30 Small Group	9:30 Outdoor
10:00 Toileting/Snack	10:20 Toileting/Snack
10:20 Outdoor	10:40 Large Group
10:50 Large Group	11:15 Dismissal
11:05 Music	
11:15 Dismissal	

These schedules show that adding Spark to the daily routine simplifies the day, with story time, small-group activities, music, and social times all integrated into the Spark hour. The schedule has become more efficient.

What is included in the Spark hour?

- Large-group story time
- Introduction to centers
- Centers (small-group activities)

Story Time

Most preschool programs include a time for reading stories to the children. This time may occur at the beginning or the end of the day. However, story time typically is not included in the program as an integral part of the day's planned activities. Teachers may caution children to "put on their listening ears" and be quiet, missing a golden opportunity for developing language skills, relating stories to children's home experiences, and teaching recall and memory skills.

Storytelling activities that involve children in discussion strengthen children's early literacy skills. The Spark story time is designed to encourage child participation. The same story is read every day of the week, and all activities for the day are based on a concept that has been drawn from the story. Children are encouraged to become both physically and verbally involved in the stories as they chant repeated sentences from the story and use physical gestures to help them understand concepts such as *rubbing*. They chant and rub their hands together to phrases that occur in the story: "The little cricket rubbed his wings together. But nothing happened. Not a sound" (see the *Very Quiet Cricket* unit). Teachers can also draw children into the story by encouraging them to relate the story to home experiences, predict what will happen next, or recall what happened in the story.

A story description in English and Spanish is included with each unit to enable teachers to send home information about the story of the week. Each description includes a brief summary of the story, an interactive question (and answer) to initiate discussion with the child, and a list of the themes of the week.

Small-Group Activities

Many classrooms have small-group activities to help children develop both general and individual skills. Too often these activities require an inordinate amount of teacher preparation time, the teacher is not present during the activity, and the children spend little time engaged in the activity. The result is that little learning takes place. The Spark curriculum requires that an adult (teacher or assistant) be present throughout the center (small-group) activities.

During an activity, the adult addresses children's individual and general goals, discusses the activity with the children, praises their efforts, and models the activity. The involvement of an adult extends children's engagement time and increases opportunities for learning.

Creative Arts Activities

Most preschool classrooms have an easel set up for children to use, art supplies readily available, and planned visual art activities. Teachers also gather the children together to sing songs and move to music. The music activities often take place when the teachers and children are waiting for something else to happen—waiting for the bus, waiting for snack, waiting for everyone to finish washing hands. It is important to have art supplies available and to sing songs with preschool children. However, if the teacher views arts activities as tools to promote skill development, the activities will become more than a time for fun. They will become times when teachers and children alike explore materials and sounds, discuss concepts, and develop skills.

The Spark arts activities are developmentally appropriate for young children. The music and movement activities provide opportunities to explore sound and to explore concepts such as *fast/slow, loud/quiet,* and *big/little.* They provide opportunities for children to move to different kinds of music and hear music from different cultures. The visual art activities provide opportunities to explore colors, textures, structures, and concepts, and to develop skills in drawing lines or shapes. The make-believe activities allow children to pretend to be characters in the story, to move like animals, to make animal sounds, and to experience social interactions.

It is critical that a program meet the needs of all children in an inclusive setting. Creative arts activities provide opportunities for all children to succeed at their own developmental levels. As one administrator of a program implementing the Spark curriculum said, "What I like about this curriculum is that there is something in it for everyone."

Learning to Use the Curriculum

Teachers trained to teach the curriculum will make the best use of what Spark has to offer, and that is the purpose of this book. These workshops inform teachers about the teaching potential of literature, music and movement, art, and make-believe, and they suggest successful methods for teaching through these areas. The workshops also introduce the curriculum and give teachers a chance to practice the teaching strategies and to become familiar with the format and the activities.

How Children Learn through Spark

Literature, music and movement, art, and drama offer many opportunities for learning. The Spark curriculum capitalizes on the inherent teachability of children's literature and the arts with activities that promote early childhood developmental skills in a wide range of learning areas: fine motor, gross motor, language, cognition, and social. Each area of the arts promotes these developmental skills in different ways and to different degrees.

Literature

Stories offer a wealth of opportunities for children to learn language and concepts and gain social knowledge. While adults can find it tedious to read and reread the same stories, children thrive on the repetition of words and story lines. As they listen to familiar stories,

they are able to absorb lessons in language, cognition, and social skills—lessons in which they are actively involved at the preschool age.

In the Spark curriculum the teacher reads the same story each day for a week as a basis for the arts activities. This daily rereading of the story provides cohesion to the week and has the potential to promote child growth in the following areas:

- Increased memory skills
- Generalization of information
- Increased attention span
- Expanded vocabulary
- Acquisition of new concepts
- Use of more complex sentence structures
- Relation of information to the child's experiences

Teachers are encouraged to make the Spark stories as enticing as possible by using a variety of voice inflections and facial expressions to match the characters. They can use hand movements when appropriate (such as moving one hand up and down and around to reinforce directional concepts) and show props (such as a magician's wand for the story *Abiyoyo* (Seeger, 1986). Teachers are also encouraged to ask questions that prompt children to think about the actions and concepts in a story.

While children should listen carefully to the story and not interrupt constantly, the teacher encourages them to be actively involved in appropriate ways during Spark story time. She might have them do hand or body movements and chant repeated phrases, such as clapping their hands during *Chicka Chicka Boom Boom* (Martin Jr. 1989) and chanting the repeated phrase "chicka chicka boom boom" whenever it occurs in the story. By being actively involved in these ways, children attend better during a story and learn new concepts faster.

Art

The Spark curriculum promotes the belief that in early childhood the process of creating art is more important than the artwork that is produced. Consequently, teachers are encouraged to model the use of materials, for example, how to dip an object in paint and then stamp it on paper to make a print. However, they are discouraged from creating a model for children to copy. Rather, teachers allow children to experiment with materials and work at their individual levels. Teachers prompt the children to try skills they are ready to attempt, for example, encouraging a child to cut out a circle she wants to paste on a collage.

Teachers become actively involved during Spark art activities in order to model skills the children are ready to try, promote individual goals, and help the children stay interested in the activity for longer periods of time. If children enjoy painting or creating structures in the art center, teachers can encourage skill development by working beside them, modeling how to make shapes, mix colors, or make very tall or short structures. As teachers model an activity, they are promoting development of the child's skills as the child is engaged in the activity. Children will have opportunities to increase their fine-motor skills as they manipulate materials, their language skills as they describe their work, and their social skills as they share materials and plan structures with other children. Children will also be able to increase cognitive skills as they solve problems and learn to point to or label colors and shapes. They will broaden their base of knowledge while they learn new concepts.

The primary skill area children practice during art activities is fine motor. Most of the fine-motor skills are considered prereading and prewriting skills. Art is an enticing way for children to practice these skills. Children also have opportunities to practice skills in language and cognition as they talk about what they are doing, learn the names of colors, count materials, and create sequential patterns with materials. They will be able to practice skills when they compare materials that are different sizes and shapes, or solve a practical problem such as how to stick plastic pieces to a box. Social skills promoted during visual arts activities include sharing space and materials, taking turns, making choices, working on projects with one or more children, following rules about using materials, and cleaning up.

Music and Movement

The music component of many preschool programs serves as a group social time, a transition activity, or a way to fill brief empty times in the school day. By contrast, music is a vital part of the Spark curriculum. In the Spark curriculum, children are actively involved in music as they experiment with materials and the sounds they make, think of new ways to move their bodies, and practice a wide range of skills. The Spark music and movement activity is used as an engaging opportunity to promote children's skills.

In order for a music program to be effective, the activities and music must be developmentally appropriate for the children in the group. Spark activities have been carefully developed to ensure that they are developmentally appropriate for young children and that they contain opportunities to promote many skills. The focus of the Spark music activities is on exploring sounds, moving to music, and singing simple songs that contain word and melodic repetition.

The primary skill areas that music and movement activities address are language, social, and gross motor. However, as the children participate in the Spark music and movement activities, they also engage in problem-solving (what materials should I put in the can to make a loud sound?), kindergarten-readiness (what shape is the drum? the maraca? the triangle?), creative (how else can I move to the music?), fine-motor, and leadership skills. Developmentally appropriate music activities for preschool children should consist of one or all three of the following components: sound exploration, movement, or simple songs.

Sound Exploration

Examples of developmentally appropriate exploratory sound activities include the following:

- Comparing the sound of big and little instruments such as drums, bells, triangles, and tambourines.

- Deciding which sounds are the same and which are different. When you drum on the table, does it sound the same as when you drum on the floor?

- Placing items such as pebbles, marbles, rice, or beans in containers and listening to the resulting sound. Compare sounds when different items are placed inside.

- Experimenting with instruments. Which ones make loud sounds, and which ones make quiet sounds?

- Experimenting with various materials. What sounds can be made with dry leaves? What sounds can be made with paper? What do you hear when you drop a cotton ball? What do you hear when you drop a rock? Which sound is louder?

Movement Activities

Drums and tambourines are excellent instruments for introducing movement to young children. The beat can be adapted to meet the needs of individual children in the classroom and should be tailored to match the motor control of the children in the room. Early in the year a simple, steady, walking drum rhythm is more appropriate than recorded music for young children to move to. The person who

is creating the beat may accent (hit harder) the first of four beats, then repeat the sequence of one hard beat followed by three lighter beats. The adult should observe the children carefully and match the beat to their motor abilities. Later, a running or tiptoeing beat may be added. The children will soon choose to tiptoe to a light beat. Finally, the teacher can try an uneven pattern to which a child may gallop or skip. Children enjoy activities that allow them to decide how to move to different rhythms, to be the leaders for other children to follow, and to decide which body parts to move.

Children also enjoy moving to recorded music. Classroom teachers should move beyond the children's records that tell children precisely how to move and should play all types of recorded music, including jazz, blues, classical, and popular, encouraging children to respond to the music in their own way. The preschool music library should include a mixture of music that is slow, fast, low, high, loud, and quiet, as well as music from different cultures.

Songs

Songs for preschool children should be selected carefully. Young children learn through repetition. Developmentally appropriate songs have repeated melody lines, repeated words, and a small number of different tones. Songs that contain wide skips in the melody should be avoided. If teachers sing a song in a key that is comfortable for them, it is probably all right for the children. However, if a teacher starts a song that the children know and they seem unable to join in, the teacher should try singing it higher or lower.

Many of the songs that are written especially for young children are not developmentally appropriate. If the adult has difficulty learning and remembering a song, it is probably not an appropriate song to use with preschoolers. Such traditional songs as "Mary Had a Little Lamb,"

"Skip to My Lou," "Here We Go Looby Lou," and "Old MacDonald" can all be used successfully in preschool classrooms. Traditional songs have been sung for many generations because they have repeated melody lines, word repetition, and easily learned melody lines. They are easy to remember and fun to sing.

Make-Believe

Dramatic-play or make-believe activities help children develop cognitive skills, social skills, self-help skills, gross-motor skills, fine-motor skills, and verbal skills. Preliteracy skills can also be enhanced by providing paper and pencil for children to use as they act out the part of a waitress, a mother writing a grocery list, a doctor writing a prescription, or even a police officer writing out a ticket.

The Spark curriculum includes the following three types of make-believe activities:

1. Children act out familiar situations, such as putting babies to bed.

2. Children manipulate figures, such as toy farm animals in a sandbox.

3. Children imitate characters or act out stories from the Spark curriculum.

Drama activities in which children act out the stories are valuable because they help children learn how to take on the role of a character and act out a theme. They can then apply these skills as they take on the roles of people in their lives in more unstructured dramatic play during free choice time. Drama activities can actually help children learn how to be more active participants during dramatic play.

During drama activities, children are directly involved in a situation that allows them to interact with each other. If needed, teachers can join in and model dramatic-play techniques. This is most appropriate when a child is ready for a more advanced level of play but needs encouragement. Teachers may also model how

to interact with others or suggest ways for children to interact: "Josh, maybe you could help Lana feed the babies." When appropriate, the teacher can also ask open-ended questions to help children expand their play: "What else does a waitress do?" "How could the doctor help her feel better?"

During Spark dramatic-play activities, the teacher joins in the play without interfering in productive interactions between children. The teacher encourages children to

- Use more advanced forms of dramatic play when they seem ready but are not progressing to the next level without teacher help.

- Attend to the play situation for longer periods of time.

- Practice new skills.

During Spark dramatic-play activities, teachers act as play partners and

- Suggest ways to expand on the scenario.

- Ask questions and make comments that encourage children to think and talk about what they are doing, interact more with each other, and think of ways to extend the activity.

- Model new skills, such as printing words for a sign or dressing a doll.

- Encourage children to interact.

Creating a Classroom Where All Children Can Learn

The Spark curriculum encourages teachers to create a classroom environment where all children experience learning as a positive and rewarding endeavor.

Each child enters a classroom already influenced by many factors—family makeup, cultural heritage, innate strengths and weaknesses, previous experiences, and sometimes disabilities. No classroom has a completely homogeneous group of children, so it is essential for teachers to create an environment of acceptance for all cultures, all types of families, and all ability levels. Spark promotes an optimal learning environment of acceptance and inclusiveness through attention to materials, attitudes, and experiences that affect the environment.

Goals for Promoting an Environment of Acceptance

An environment of acceptance starts with some general goals for the children in a classroom. Goals help adults plan the materials they will use as well as the attitudes they will promote. Such goals might include the following:

- To respect all cultures and values.
- To function successfully in a multicultural, multi-ability world.
- To develop a positive self-concept.
- To view differences and similarities among people in positive ways.
- To experience a whole community as made up of all kinds of people.

Materials That Promote Acceptance

The materials used in a classroom can communicate a strong message of acceptance. Books should picture people from a variety of cultures in everyday life situations and should avoid stereotypes. They should contain both males and females, with and without disabilities, in active, varied roles. Fortunately, the publishing industry is responding to this need and every year there are more books available that are conducive to an unbiased environment. The Spark curriculum includes books that reflect this inclusive message of acceptance.

Music can represent a wide range of backgrounds and tastes. Music should be authentic,

that is, recorded music played on instruments from the culture where the music originated. Music suggested for use in Spark activities reflects this respect for the authenticity and variety in music.

Young children are generally more accepting of all types of music than older children and adults who have been influenced by their own culture and the familiarity of the music they hear most often. Consequently, adults are often surprised to see young children enjoying and moving to music that the adults had hesitated to use in the classrooms. To maintain the children's enthusiasm for a variety of music, adults should try not to show their own negative reactions to unfamiliar musical sounds.

Adults may also teach the children songs from a range of cultures. Folk songs are the most likely to succeed because even if they are sung in a foreign language, they often have repeating lyrics and repeated melodic lines that are developmentally appropriate for young children.

Attitudes and Experiences That Promote Acceptance

An environment of acceptance in a classroom only exists if the adults in the classroom are open to the different types of family situations and cultural backgrounds of the children with whom they work. Adults may need to look at their own attitudes toward people who are different from them, and be willing to learn about the cultures children experience at home. See appendix 3 for a list of other resources to enable teachers to assess their cultural awareness.

Different cultural experiences should be a welcome part of classroom discussions and make-believe play. What is most meaningful to preschool children is the world they encounter directly every day. They learn about themselves and their world by talking about their experiences with each other and acting them out in play.

For example, while listening to a story, children may discuss their own experiences and discover that everyone does not live in exactly the same way. By encouraging children to tell about their own lives, the teacher ensures that everyone is getting a firsthand lesson in social studies in a way that promotes a feeling of acceptance for each person's uniqueness.

Cultural differences may be very evident during make-believe play when children act out behaviors and lifestyles that are most familiar to them. Children establish their own cultural identity during make-believe play by imitating behaviors of the adults they are closest to. When children play together they also discover that while cultures might differ, the basics of family life and interactions among people are more similar than different.

Teaching Strategies That Promote Acceptance

While different cultural and personal factors have an effect on children and the way they learn, there are some teaching strategies that work well with preschool children from all types of homes and with a wide range of abilities. These strategies are effective because they reflect the nature of young children and how they learn. When the Spark teaching strategies were developed, input was sought from a wide variety of sources that included professionals in the field and parents from many cultures. An analysis of the data identified the following strategies as best practice, and are those used by the Spark curriculum:

- Teach through hands-on activities.
- Use a blend of modeling and direct teaching.
- Allow children to work in small groups.
- Provide open-ended materials and activities.
- Embed children's goals in high-interest activities.
- Integrate skills from various domains in high-interest activities.
- Allow children to make choices.
- Ask questions that promote thinking and learning.

Providing Feedback to Staff

Administrative staff need to understand that the work of the teaching staff is intensive during the first year that they implement the Spark curriculum. Teaching assistants may have a role that is very different from the one they usually play in the classroom. Both the teacher and the teaching assistant teach small-group activities. The teaching team learns to use new teaching strategies and tools (music and movement, art, and make-believe) that may be new to them. In addition, they are working with new curricular materials. They need positive feedback, yet they also must know when changes should be made in what they are doing.

The most successful techniques for providing feedback to teaching staff include

- Regular observations of the classroom using an Observation Checklist (see appendix 1). The purpose of these observations is to determine how the curriculum is being implemented in the classroom and the areas in which the teaching team may need additional training. These observations should be scheduled with teachers ahead of time.

- Regular meetings with the teaching staff as a whole. The purpose of these meetings is to provide a forum for teachers to share information with each other and for the administrator to give general information to the staff.

- Regular meetings with each teaching team. The purpose of these meetings is to provide additional training as needed and to meet the specific needs of the team. These needs will have been identified through the observations and through teacher self-evaluation.

- Videotapes for self-evaluation. Videos can be taken in the classroom periodically and given to the teaching team for self-evaluation. The team should be given reflective questions to use as they observe the tape. Their responses to the questions and their perceptions of their own teaching can then be discussed during a team meeting.

See appendix 1 for forms used in the Spark observation and feedback process.

Refresher Training

Teachers may have difficulty assimilating all of the strategies suggested by the Spark curriculum in their first year of implementation. The teaching strategies that are an integral part of the curriculum may require that teachers make changes in their teaching style. Feeling comfortable with such changes takes time. Refresher training at the beginning of the second year of implementation helps teachers renew their enthusiasm for teaching through the arts and pick up the strategies that they have not yet fully made a part of their teaching style.

One way to pinpoint the level of training and the areas in which additional training is needed is to use the Observation Checklist several times at the end of the first year of implementation and again at the beginning of the new year to observe and record how each teacher is implementing the curriculum. Compare the observations and then tailor the refresher training to fit the needs of the teachers.

If the teachers are receiving high marks on the Observation Checklist, no additional training is needed. However, if any of the following needs are identified by the observations, additional training is indicated:

- Discussion of the stories seldom includes open-ended questions.

- Praise consists of "good job" without specifying what the child has done well.

- The teacher does not demonstrate center activities before the children make choices.

- The teacher seldom addresses children's individual skills during the activities.

Typical examples of where teachers may be after a few months of implementation follow.

Story Reading

Skills the teacher has acquired:

- Reads the story in an interesting manner.

- Has the children chant repeated sections as suggested in the activity.

- Encourages the children to make hand gestures as suggested in the activity.

- Goes back through the story, asking test questions.

Skills that need improvement:

- Drawing children into discussion of the story.

- Asking open-ended questions.

- Relating the story to the child's home experiences.

- Paraphrasing complex stories.

Introduction of Center Activities

Skills the teacher has acquired:

- Tells children which centers will be open.

- Permits children to choose which center they want to attend.

- Tells what will happen in the center: "You will move to music and make sounds with instruments in the music center."

Skills that need improvement:

- Demonstrating the activity (playing a short segment of the tape and having a child show how to move or how to make a sound with an instrument).

- Teaching new skills that are part of the activity.

- Making the activity enticing to the children.

Teacher Involvement in the Center Activity

Skills the teacher has acquired:

- Prepares before the activity begins.

- Typically follows the Spark activity as presented.

- Is present during the activity.

- Relates the activity to the theme of the day.

Skills that need improvement:

- Promoting children's general and individual skill development during the activities.

- Modeling the activity.

- Asking open-ended questions.

- Teaching through positive reinforcement.

Suggestions for Conducting Spark Workshops

Because everyone who works in a given classroom will be involved with the Spark approach, it's important that all members of a classroom teaching team attend the workshop together. This includes aides, assistant teachers, teachers, and head teachers, and may also include regular parent volunteers if they will be helping to implement the program. If speech, occupational, or physical therapists or other specialists work with the children, they should also be invited to attend the workshop. Seat teaching teams together for the workshops, since some of the exercises will require that they work together.

The Spark workshops are presented in separate modules to enable facilitators to fit them into their individual in-service training schedules. The first workshop, The Spark Curriculum,

takes a full day. The arts workshops are presented as separate half-day workshops; however, the in-service training is most effective when it is presented in two full, consecutive days.

Facilitators who plan to provide two consecutive days of in-service can adapt the arts training workshops in the following manner:

- Present the informational section of each workshop.

- Break for lunch.

- Implement the small-group arts activities, Learning to Teach and Adapt Spark.

Instead of having the teachers practice implementing four of the center activities from the Art, Make-Believe, and Music and Movement workshops, select one activity from each of the arts workshops, e.g., one from the Art Workshop, one from the Make-Believe Workshop, and one from the Music and Movement Workshop. If the number of participants warrants breaking into more than three small groups, choose two activities from one of the workshops.

Overheads and handouts for each workshop are included at the end of the workshop; overhead numbers begin with the workshop number, so that to conduct workshop 2, for example, the instructor will need all overheads numbered in the 200s. Note that the Child Goals handout is in appendix 2; it is needed for workshops 2, 3, and 4. Program evaluation forms, used in workshop 5, are all in appendix 1.

Summary

The Spark curriculum has been implemented and found to be effective with more than six thousand children and their families in many types of programs, including family child care, community day care, Head Start, inclusive public school programs, and self-contained early childhood special education classrooms. Teachers have used the materials in ways that best fit the needs of their programs. Many have adapted the activities to meet the individual needs of children, used the Activity Matrixes as lesson plans, and sent home the Skills and Their Underlying Goals and Objectives to show parents what skills their children will be working on during a given week. The curriculum is a tool for teachers to use and enjoy.

Many preschool teachers spend an inordinate amount of time looking for new materials for their classrooms because they must develop their own curriculum. The Spark curriculum is a field-tested tool that teachers can use to promote child growth. The emphasis is on highly engaging, open-ended activities that require no specific product. This format provides opportunities for all children to learn and achieve success at their individual levels.

Administrators have found that the Spark curriculum meets the needs of their programs. They report that it does not increase their work; instead, the time they spend in the preschool program is more efficiently used. They say that it brings consistency to their preschool programs and that when they observe in classrooms, they know what to expect. One school principal reported, "When I observed in the classroom, I was surprised that such young children could be so involved. They didn't even know that I was there. They came from such diverse backgrounds and yet they were all so involved together."

Our intent is to help teachers meet the needs of all the children in the inclusive classroom. We expect teachers to choose the units that best fit their schedule, choose activities for each day of the week to promote the concept of the day, and adapt the activities to meet the needs of the children in their room. We hope that teachers and children alike will have fun as they learn with Spark.

WORKSHOP 1
The Spark Curriculum

I. Instructions for the Spark Trainer

II. Training Script

Introduction to the Spark Curriculum (20 minutes)

The Creative Arts Curriculum (60 minutes)

Break (10 minutes)

Teaching Strategies (50 minutes)

Teaching the Center Activities (50 minutes)

Lunch

Story Time (90 minutes)

Creating an Environment of Acceptance (30 minutes)

Fitting Spark into the Lesson Plan (30 minutes)

Summary (20 minutes)

III. Handouts

IV. Overheads

I. Instructions for the Spark Trainer

Purpose

The purpose of this workshop is to help teachers learn how to implement the Spark Curriculum for Early Childhood. They will receive a brief explanation of the curriculum and the premise upon which it is based. They will learn how children's skills can be addressed in all five domains (gross motor, fine motor, cognitive, language, and social) during the center activities. Teachers will become familiar with the format of the curriculum and with teaching strategies that will help children acquire skills and understand concepts. They will practice embedding targeted goals in Spark units and will understand how the Spark curriculum helps create a classroom environment where all children feel comfortable and eager to learn. Finally, they will be given suggestions about how other teachers have fit Spark into their classroom routine.

Preparing for the Workshop

The following preparations will help make the workshop a success. Trainers should read through the instructions at least twice.

☐ Gather materials listed for the workshop.

☐ Prepare overheads.

☐ Make copies of handouts that are provided for the workshop. Place handouts in folders with names of participants on the front.

☐ Make cards for the Adapting Activities small-group demonstration (see below).

☐ Recruit a participant to introduce one of the centers during the *Abiyoyo* demonstration (see page 21).

☐ Set up the room with a space in front of the audience for demonstrations.

☐ Set up cans and strikers for the role-play.

☐ Seat teaching teams together by placing handout folders on the tables before the session begins. This seating arrangement enables all members of a teaching team to begin thinking of the implementation as a team effort and helps them work as a team throughout the training.

☐ Mark suggested pages in storybooks with paper clips.

☐ Set up overhead projector.

☐ Enjoy the workshop!

Materials to Be Prepared and Gathered

☐ Overheads 101 through 146

☐ Handouts (see next page)

☐ Blank transparencies and transparency marker, or flip chart and marker

☐ Spark books (see below)

☐ Six empty cans with lids and strikers (cans of various sizes and strikers of different materials, such as metal spoons, sticks, rhythm sticks)

☐ One set of the Spark activity books for each pair of participants

☐ Bell and striker (resonator bell if available; triangle or cymbal could be substituted)

☐ Magician's cape or piece of fabric

☐ Rolled piece of paper to represent a magician's wand

☐ Bubble solution and wand

☐ Paintbrush

☐ Small container of water

☐ Heavy piece of paper to use as a fan

Spark Books

☐ *Abiyoyo*

☐ *Anansi and the Moss-Covered Rock*

☐ *Baby Rattlesnake*

☐ *I Need a Lunch Box*

☐ *Jonathan and His Mommy*

☐ *Mama, Do You Love Me?*

☐ *No Fair to Tigers*

☐ *The Napping House*

☐ *Tree of Cranes*

Note: The number of activity matrixes you need will depend on the number of participants in the training. For example, if there are fewer than ten participants, you will only need to prepare three activities from this list (choose one each of art, music and movement, and make-believe), and you will only need to copy the activity pages and matrixes that correspond to that unit.

Handouts

☐ Spark Story Chart—one for each participant

☐ Activity Matrix from the *Abiyoyo* unit—one for each participant

☐ One copy each of the Activity Matrixes for the following units:

   ☐ *Anansi and the Moss-Covered Rock*

   ☐ *Big Al*

   ☐ *The Little Mouse, the Red Ripe Strawberry, and the Big Hungry Bear*

   ☐ *The Bossy Gallito*

   ☐ *The Tree of Cranes*

   ☐ *The Very Quiet Cricket*

☐ One copy each of the following activity pages:

   ☐ *Abiyoyo*, Day 1, Art

   ☐ *Anansi and the Moss-Covered Rock*, Day 1, Art

   ☐ *Big Al*, Day 1, Art

   ☐ *Big Al*, Day 2, Art

   ☐ *The Little Mouse, the Red Ripe Strawberry, and the Big Hungry Bear*, Day 3, Music and Movement

   ☐ *The Bossy Gallito*, Day 3, Music and Movement

   ☐ *The Little Mouse, the Red Ripe Strawberry, and the Big Hungry Bear*, Day 3, Make-Believe

   ☐ *The Tree of Cranes*, Day 2, Music and Movement

   ☐ *The Very Quiet Cricket*, Day 3, Make-Believe

   ☐ *The Very Quiet Cricket*, Day 1, Art

☐ Teaching through the Activity worksheets, one for each team

☐ Implementing the Spark Curriculum handout, one for each participant

Cards for Adapting Activities Demonstration

Write the following text on individual file cards to be handed out to teams:

☐ *Abiyoyo*, Day 1, Art (disappear) (child with visual limitations)

- *Anansi and the Moss-Covered Rock,* Day 1, Art (covered) (child with social needs, or child with limited fine-motor abilities)

- *Big Al,* Day 1, Art (ocean) (child who cannot label specific colors, child who is tactilely defensive)

- *The Little Mouse, the Red Ripe Strawberry, and the Big Hungry Bear,* Day 3, Music and Movement (half) (child with cognitive limitations, ESL child)

- *The Bossy Gallito,* Day 3, Music and Movement (dirty/clean) (hyperactive child, non-ambulatory child)

- *The Little Mouse, the Red Ripe Strawberry, and the Big Hungry Bear,* Day 3, Make-Believe (half) (child who can't manipulate scissors, child who has cognitive limitations)

- *The Tree of Cranes,* Day 2, Music and Movement (hot/cold) (deaf child, child with challenging behaviors)

- *The Very Quiet Cricket,* Day 3, Make-Believe (together) (child with weak grasp, child with limited use of his hands)

- *Big Al,* Day 2, Art (child who cannot work with others, blind child)

- *The Very Quiet Cricket,* Day 1, Art (child with limited motor control, child with limited English)

II. Training Script

Introduction to the Spark Curriculum

Tell the participants that the workshop will provide an introduction to the Spark curriculum and the methods used by the curriculum to promote the widely diverse skills of children. Give them time to read through the overhead.

Show OH (overhead) 101, Goals of the Spark Workshop.

Goals of Spark

Display the overhead Goals of Spark. Briefly explain that in order to reach the goals listed on the overhead, Spark uses a set of teaching strategies and a culturally diverse curriculum based on literacy and on the arts, including music, visual art, and make-believe.

Show OH 102, Goals of Spark.

Show OH 103, Premise.

State that the premise of Spark is that all children's skills can be promoted through a combination of children's stories and the arts. Extensive field-testing in a variety of settings indicates that the Spark activities are highly interesting to young children and that teachers are able to address children's goals through the activities.

Show OH 104, Components of the Spark Curriculum.

State that there are three components of Spark: the creative arts curriculum, staff training, and family involvement. Discuss each component briefly as you show the following overheads:

Show OH 105a and 105b, Characteristics of Spark Activities.

Characteristics of Spark Activities

Name the five domains (gross motor, fine motor, cognitive, language, and social) and explain that the curriculum addresses each through a number of activities.

Show OH 106, Cultural Diversity; refer to Story Chart handout.

Cultural Diversity

Point out that the books used in the curriculum represent many cultures and that the teaching strategies suggested by the curriculum provide opportunities for all children to succeed. Tell them to look at the handout of the Spark Story Chart. It provides a comprehensive view of all the stories used in the curriculum.

Show OH 107, Family Materials.

Family Materials

Explain that the family materials are sent home each week and include the story descriptions. The purpose is to keep the family informed about what is going on in the classroom and to enable them to discuss the weekly story with their child.

Show OH 108, The Spark Curriculum.

The Spark Curriculum

With overhead 108 displayed, provide time for the participants to read the definition. Say that the primary purpose of the activities is to promote child growth. The goal is not to teach the arts but to use arts activities as vehicles to promote children's skill development.

Format of the Weekly Unit

Explain that the Spark curriculum takes approximately an hour a day to implement.

Show OH 109, The Spark Curriculum.

Explain that the Spark hour begins with a large-group activity that lasts between twenty and thirty minutes. It is followed by simultaneous center activities, based on the arts, that last approximately thirty minutes. Children flow from one center to the other. It takes about fifteen minutes for a child to complete each center activity—however, children may stay at one center for the entire center time if they wish. Each center activity is repeated at least once to give all the children the opportunity to participate in all the centers.

Each week consists of a unit based on a story that the teacher reads every day. Each day's activities are based on a unifying theme (such as *ocean*) or concept (such as *disappear*) that has been drawn from the story.

Teachers reinforce the themes and concepts and embed children's goals both in story time and in the center activities that follow story time. At the activity centers, children are in small groups as they engage in music, visual art, and make-believe (dramatic play) activities.

With overhead 110 showing, point out that each day's activities have been developed on the theme of the day. Talk through the matrix, stressing that the theme or concept of the day was drawn out of the story. The purpose of the theme is twofold: to broaden children's knowledge base, and to unify the day's activities. Invite the participants to look at the *Abiyoyo* activity matrix handout. Ask them what other concepts are addressed during the week. Ask someone to tell you what the music activity is for day 4. Help them to understand the layout of the matrix.

Show OH 110, Abiyoyo Matrix. Discuss Activity Matrix handout.

With overhead 111 showing, discuss embedded teaching strategies. Say that these are all critical components of the curriculum, and ask if anyone has questions, comments, or concerns. Many teachers have reservations about repeating the same story daily. State that this strategy has proven to be one of the most effective strategies used in the curriculum and that it will be discussed in detail later.

Show OH 111, Embedded Teaching Strategies.

Spark Format: Day 1

Say that the organization of the Spark hour will be familiar to many teachers: large-group story-reading time followed by small-group center time.

Show OH 112a, Spark Unit Organization

With overhead 112a showing, explain that all the Spark units are organized in the same way. Ask each teaching team to look at the *Abiyoyo* unit in Volume 1 of the Spark Activities. Say that you will use this unit to discuss the format of the curriculum because it is an all-time favorite of children and teachers who have used the curriculum. Mention that the story is one of the most complex in the curriculum. Most children will not be ready for this unit at the beginning of the year. Encourage participants to follow the steps in the Abiyoyo unit as each section is discussed.

Introduce *Abiyoyo* **unit.**

Ask participants to follow format.

Show OH 112b.

Show OH 113, Spark Activity Format, Day 1. Explain "Read the story" section.

Show *Abiyoyo* pages with song and "Zoop."

Explain next section, "Discuss the story."

Introduce *disappear.* Show *Abiyoyo* page where the giant has disappeared.

Blow bubbles and make them disappear.

With OH 112b showing, say that each Spark unit is made up of the same pieces. The first is an introduction to the story upon which the unit is based. This introduction is for the teacher's use. It provides a synopsis of the story, suggests how a teacher might use it in the classroom, presents special issues that the teacher might want to consider, and tells the teacher if any unusual materials are required to complete the unit. Following the introduction is a chart called the Activity Matrix, which shows the week's activities and the concepts upon which each day's curriculum is based. The main section of the unit, the daily curricular activities, is next. After that is a list of some of the skills that can be promoted during the week. The unit closes with a handout in both English and Spanish about the week's story to send home for families.

With overhead 113 showing, explain the activity format.

First step: Read the story. Start with the first section of day 1, which is "Read the story." Explain that the teacher begins each unit by reading the story of the week to the entire group of children. Emphasize once again that it is critical for the teacher to read the story every day of the week, because the unit is based on the story. Story repetition is one of the basic strategies of the curriculum.

The teacher promotes attending and learning during story time by promoting discussion about the story and by encouraging children to be physically and verbally involved. Give an example from *Abiyoyo*. Show the book. Say that this story offers several opportunities for child involvement, such as the *Abiyoyo* song and the repeated "Zoop" when the father makes something disappear.

Second step: Discuss the story. Explain that discussion of the story is encouraged in order to give children an opportunity to express opinions, relate personal experiences, and increase language skills. Ideas for the discussion are included in the activity outline.

Third step: Introduce the concept. Explain that after reading and discussing the story, the teacher uses a short group activity to introduce the concept of the day. State that whenever possible, the concepts should be connected to the book and should be physically demonstrated for the children.

Show the book *Abiyoyo* and turn to the page on which the father uses his magic wand to make the giant disappear. Explain that the concept of the day is *disappear,* introduced by using a bottle of bubble solution.

Blow some bubbles with the solution and then clap your hands on a bubble. Say that the bubble disappeared. Engage the participants by having one of them clap hands on a bubble. Say that this visual demonstration helps children understand the concept and makes the abstract concept of *disappear* concrete.

Fourth step: Introduce the centers. Say that the Spark curriculum includes small-group center activities for the first four days of the week. Each center consists of either music and movement, art, or make-believe activities that are related to the story by the unifying concept of the day. By participating in the activities in each center, the children strengthen their understanding of the concept through multisensory experiences. They also practice a variety of kindergarten-readiness skills. There should be one adult at each of the centers to work with the children; a teaching assistant can take on an active teaching role. In some programs, the speech therapist or another staff member leads one of the centers.

There may be two or three centers for the children to choose from, depending on the number of adults present in the classroom. Explain that the centers are most successful if the children are in small groups of not more than six.

Explain that the teacher models the activities that will take place in each center. This is his opportunity to demonstrate any new skills that will be used in the activity and to show the children what they will be doing in the activity. Research suggests that many children do not learn to make choices in early childhood programs. This becomes a disadvantage when they enter kindergarten. Therefore, it is a valuable teaching strategy to provide opportunities for children to learn to choose activities, materials, and what to do with the materials. The Spark curriculum encourages teachers to invite children to choose the center they will attend first. After the first center, the children will flow into the second center. Since the children choose the first center, the centers should be introduced in a manner that is both informative and enticing.

Model introducing a music center and a make-believe center. (It is more interesting to the participants if you ask someone else to be prepared to introduce one of the centers. Use the *Abiyoyo* day 1 activities since this is the unit that is being used to introduce the format of the curriculum to the participants.) Demonstrate through your introductions to the centers the difference between simply stating the name of the center and demonstrating what the children will do in each center. For example, first say, "Today the music center will be open." Have the helper say, "Today the make-believe center will be open." (Notice that you have given the participants some information, but you have not

Introduce centers; explain staffing.

Show how *not* to introduce centers.

Introduce music center as in *Abiyoyo* **unit, using bell.**

Have assistant introduce make-believe as in *Abiyoyo* **unit, using cape and bubbles.**

Show OH 114, Introducing Center Activities, and **OH 115,** The Importance of Center Introduction. Explain why the second approach is better.

Show OH 116, The Purpose of Center Activity.

Show OH 117, Spark Center Activities.

Show OH 118, Using Arts Activities.

Use blank transparencies; brainstorm skills.

told two important things: what will happen in the center and how the term "disappear" will be used to tie the center activities to the story. You have also not made the introduction enticing.) Ask participants to choose the center in which they wish to participate based on this information alone.

Now introduce the centers as described in the curriculum. Strike a bell or another instrument that vibrates after it is struck and immediately stop the vibrations with your hand. Say, "I made the sound disappear like the father in the story made things disappear!" Make the sound again. Invite a participant to make the sound disappear. Tell the participants that today in the music center they will make sounds disappear on the musical instruments.

Have your helper put on the cape, make bubbles, and use the magic wand to burst the bubbles. The helper should say, "I'm a magician like the boy's father in *Abiyoyo,* and I made the bubbles disappear!" and then tell what will happen in the make-believe center. Now ask the participants again to choose an activity center as if they were the children.

Show overhead 114. Ask participants how the two ways of introducing the centers were different. Point out that in the second example, the introductions have demonstrated what children will do in the centers, the centers have been related to the story and the concept of the day, and the activities have been shown in an enticing way. Show OH 115. Say that if the centers are introduced in an enticing way, children are much more likely to be enthusiastic about the activities. The curriculum will go more smoothly.

Spark Centers

Explain that the purpose of the center activity is to reinforce the concept of the day and to provide engaging, developmentally appropriate activities in the arts through which the teacher can promote children's skill development.

Say that the curriculum includes a center activity based on art, make-believe, and music and movement each of the first four days of the week.

State that each area of the arts has different attributes and that children learn different skills as they participate in each of these center activities. For this reason, all the areas of the arts should be used during the week.

Invite participants to brainstorm the types of skills that can be promoted in center activities in each of the arts areas. Use a blank transparency for each center, and ask participants to list the skills that they think could be developed in each. Be sure that all of the domains, gross motor, fine motor, cognitive (exploration and problem solving), language, and social (children's interactions with one another), are included in the discussion.

Say that the Spark activities provide opportunities for children to participate and succeed at their own level. They enable teachers to promote children's individual skills. They provide opportunities for children to choose materials and to choose how they will use the materials. Say that these general-readiness skills are embedded in the activities and that open-ended activities like these provide an ideal opportunity for teachers to individualize instruction for children with diverse abilities.

Explain that the period of time for center activities is at least thirty minutes, which allows for children to flow from one activity to another during the center time. Each activity is implemented twice in that time. If some children want to stay at one center throughout the entire center time, the teacher may allow them to do so, although they should participate in each type of activity during the week.

Spark Format: Days 2, 3, and 4

Ask participants to turn to day 2 of the *Abiyoyo* unit. Ask them to look at the activity carefully and tell you what is different from day 1. Point out that the formats of days 2, 3, and 4 differ from day 1 only in the review of the previous day's activities. Say that teachers have found the review to be an invaluable teaching tool. They report that it strengthens children's recall skills, improves their self-esteem, provides opportunities for group discussion, and provides an opportunity to review the concept or theme of the previous day. Give participants time to leaf through the unit.

Spark Format: Day 5

Explain that on day 5, the teacher sets up a make-believe setting that is related to the story of the week in some way. The activity may relate to one of the concepts in the story, the action in the story, or the setting in the story.

Ask participants to locate day 5 in the *Abiyoyo* unit. They will note that the theme for the day's make-believe play is *the circus*. This builds upon the fact that the father in the story is a magician.

Explain that on this day, the teacher may want to review concepts that were introduced on the previous days. Ask the participants to suggest ways that a teacher might review the concept *disappear* as the children pretend to be in a circus.

Tell the participants to take a ten-minute stretch break.

Show OH 119, Spark Format, Days 2, 3, 4; discuss; show **OH 120,** Review of Center Activities.

Show OH 121, Spark Format, Day 5.

Direct participants to *Abiyoyo* **day 5.**

Ask how teachers might relate *disappear* **to** *circus.*

Take ten-minute break.

Teaching Strategies

Show OH 122, Process over Product.

Say that young children learn by doing, and that while they are engaged in an activity, teachers can promote skill development. The finished product isn't important, but the process of making the product is very important. Prioritizing the process enables children to work at their individual levels. Say that the Spark activities have no specific end product.

Show OH 123, Teacher's Role during Center Activities.

Use overhead 123 to discuss the teacher's role during center activities, stating that in order to fulfill this role, the teacher must be present during the activity. State that the Spark curriculum encourages the teacher to use a blend of modeling and direct teaching.

Say that it takes careful planning to prepare for activities and to ensure that an adult is present during the activity to promote skill development. The next activity will demonstrate this point.

Demonstration: Music Activity without Adult Participation

Get volunteers and distribute materials.

Explain that you are going to try a couple of different ways of leading a music activity. Ask for three to five volunteers to role-play the parts of preschool children. Ask the volunteers to sit on the floor at the front of the room. Go across the room (or out of the room) to get the empty cans and strikers, telling the volunteers to sit with their legs like pretzels and put their hands in their laps. Return and pass out the empty cans (of various sizes) and strikers to each volunteer.

Leave volunteers alone.

Tell the volunteers to see what kinds of sounds they can make with their cans. Tell them that when they're finished, they can go play. Walk away and pretend to busy yourself doing something else, such as paperwork.

Return; take cans; thank volunteers.

Wait five minutes. Go back and say that it's time to clean up. Take the cans; give no praise. Thank the volunteers.

Demonstration: Spark Music and Movement Activity

Conduct Spark music and movement activity.

Now say that you are going to try another way of leading the same activity. Put the cans and strikers in the center of the area where the demonstration will be held so they are easily accessible. Ask for new volunteers to come join you and pretend to be children. Sit on the floor with the volunteers near the cans and strikers. Encourage them to choose their own cans and strikers. Comment on the sizes and colors (if appropriate) of the containers as the "children" make their choices.

Participate in the activity, in the role of "teacher," asking questions and modeling investigation of the cans and ways to make different noises with them. Include such concepts as size, color, long/short, loud/quiet, top/bottom, shapes, and body parts: "I can strike my can with my hand (fingers, thumb, elbow)."

Throughout the activity, provide positive reinforcement: "I like the way you are playing quietly." "Marcia is playing on the top of her can! What good thinking!"

After five minutes of the activity, say that it's time to clean up. Praise the "children" for their good thinking, and encourage them to help you collect the materials. Thank the volunteers for their help.

Use overhead 124 to discuss the two demonstrations. Ask participants to explain their answers to the questions.

Point out that the teacher has to be involved in order to optimize learning.

Point out that when children get their own materials, waiting time is reduced.

Show overhead 127, saying that these are the general teaching strategies used in the Spark curriculum. Ask participants for questions or observations. Use overhead 128 as a summary and discuss the teacher's role in Spark—how is it different from what the participants usually do? Ask for comments or questions.

Child Behaviors

Say that the Spark curriculum encourages children to learn through doing. Rather than using direct teaching methods and product-oriented activities, the Spark curriculum encourages the child's active participation in the learning process. The children learn to make choices about the centers they participate in, the materials they use in the centers, and how to use the materials. They participate in multisensory experiences, thus experiencing the concept of the day auditorily, visually, and through imaginative play. Instead of listening quietly to stories, the children are expected to participate actively by chanting phrases, using appropriate physical gestures, and entering into discussions. Children are encouraged to solve problems, for example, by deciding what to put into cans to make loud noises. Discuss the points on overhead 129.

Teaching the Center Activities

Say that preparation is the key to success. Say that preparing ahead to teach Spark activities is simply best teaching practice—

Model instrument playing; experiment with sounds; respond to children.

Give positive reinforcement.

End activity; thank volunteers.

Show OH 124, Discussion of Demonstration; discuss.

Show OH 125, Optimal Learning.

Show OH 126, Reduce Waiting.

Show OH 127, Teaching Strategies. **Show OH 128,** Teacher's Role in Center Activities.

Show OH 129, Teaching Strategies: Child Behaviors.

Show and discuss OH 130, Preparing Ahead: The Key to Success; **show OH 131,** Developing Children's Skills.

every good teacher prepares. Say that Spark activities are developmentally appropriate, but groups of children differ widely. The large-group story-reading activities seldom need to be adapted; however, the small-group activities may need adaptation to meet specific child needs.

Read *The Little Mouse, the Red Ripe Strawberry, and the Big Hungry Bear.*

Have everyone turn to the unit and read through the "Introducing the Story" activity.

Show OH 132, Thinking through an Activity; discuss.

Demonstration: **The Little Mouse, the Red Ripe Strawberry, and the Big Hungry Bear**

Summarize the story of *The Little Mouse, the Red Ripe Strawberry, and the Big Hungry Bear,* showing the book as you read.

Ask everyone to turn to the *Little Mouse, the Red Ripe Strawberry, and the Big Hungry Bear* unit in volume 2, or have them take out their photocopies of day 1, Group Time. Ask them to read through the "Introducing the Story" activity.

Use overhead 132 as a guide to discuss what happens in the activity. Ask participants to respond to the questions.

Remind the participants that although all the activities are developmentally appropriate, they may still need to be adapted to meet the needs of individual children. The next activity will give them the opportunity to practice adapting an activity for children with specific needs.

Say that the next exercise will be done in teams. If the group is small, you may leave people in teaching teams of two or three. If the group is large and time for reporting back is limited, you may choose to combine teams to get groups of four to six people for this activity.

Break into teams; distribute Teaching through the Activities handout and file cards; explain activity.

Assign a story and give each team a Teaching through the Activities handout, a file card with an activity and a child who needs an adaptation, and the unit matrix that accompanies that file card. Ask everyone to review the handout. Tell each group to select a leader who will record the discussion on the provided work sheet and report to the group as a whole. Say that they will have fifteen minutes to complete the activity. Tell them to use the activity matrix to see the scope of the activities for their unit for the week.

Give time to complete work-sheet; ask leaders to report back; discuss.

Give the teams fifteen to twenty minutes to think through their activities and answer the questions on the Thinking through the Activity handout. Ask each team leader to report back on their responses to the questions on the handout and to present their adaptation of the activity for the child with special needs. Encourage them to give background information such as the name of the unit and the concept of the day to put the activity in context. After each group presents, ask the other participants if they have any questions or comments. Stress again that the activities are all developmentally appropriate but that there are many different levels of skills development in the early childhood classes. Say that the activities will be most meaningful to them and the children if they plan ahead and adapt as necessary.

Ask the group to take a break for lunch.

Take lunch break.

Story Time

Reading the Story

State that story time is one of the most effective segments of the Spark curriculum; read through overhead 133. Say that story illustrations are often children's introduction to art.

Show OH 133, Importance of Reading Stories.

Say that many teachers do not involve the children when they read stories. Children may be told "to zip their mouths and turn on their ears." The Spark approach is different. Children listen better and remain more focused if they are involved in the story. For this reason, many of the Spark stories include the chanting of repeated phrases and the use of accompanying physical gestures. For example, during a reading of *The Very Quiet Cricket*, children are encouraged to rub their hands together when the little cricket rubs his wings together and join the teacher on the repeated phrase, "The little cricket rubbed his wings together. But nothing happened. Not a sound."

Show OH 134, Benefits of Involving Children at Story Time.

Say that research indicates that children also benefit in many ways from repeated readings of the same story. Read aloud the benefits listed on overhead 135a and 135b, saying that these are all benefits that have been identified by teachers.

Show OH 135a and **135b,** Value of Story Repetition.

State that since both story repetition and child verbal and physical involvement are effective teaching strategies, they are used throughout the Spark curriculum.

Show OH 136, Spark Story Time.

Story Discussion

Say that the discussion that follows the story also enhances the children's understanding of the story, promotes their language development, and enhances their social development. Discuss overhead 137. Ask for examples of open-ended questions and closed questions, what might occur during the discussion of a story (sharing of child's experiences), and what skills could be promoted when children are demonstrating actions from the story.

Show OH 137, Promoting Children's Skill Development.

Ask volunteer for boring rendition of *Anansi*.

Making the Story Interesting

Ask a volunteer to read the first six pages of *Anansi and the Moss-Covered Rock* in a very boring manner. Tell the volunteer to role-play a teacher who would rather be anyplace else and is tired of reading to children.

Say that it is obvious that if one is going to read the same story every day of the week, it must be read in an interesting manner each time.

Discuss ways to make story more interesting.

Ask participants to suggest ways to make each reading of the story more interesting. Be sure the discussion includes such suggestions as voice inflections, facial expression, hand/body movements, and props.

Ask volunteer to read same pages, using suggestions.
Show OH 138, Teachers' Comments.

Ask someone to read the same pages of the story again, using the suggestions to make the story more interesting.

Show overhead 138, and read some of the teachers' comments out loud. Provide time for participants to read through the others.

Creating an Environment of Acceptance

Use blank transparency to brainstorm differences among children.

Ask the participants to visualize the children in their classrooms. Comment that none of the children are exactly alike; they come from different home experiences and have different individual traits. Print "boys and girls" on a blank overhead transparency and say that gender is one way that the children differ. Ask the participants to think of other factors that make the children unique individuals. Their suggestions might include the following:

■ Family composition

■ Economic level

■ Ethnicity

■ Age

■ Number of siblings

■ Disabilities

■ Different types of experiences

When the list contains several traits, say that it is important to create an environment in the classroom that tells children that their own lifestyles and individual traits are accepted. Stress that it is important to show by example that it is all right to be different. Say that the Spark curriculum addresses cultural diversity in three specific ways.

The Materials in the Classroom

Stress that materials used in the classroom should encourage acceptance of differences. Say that the Spark materials encourage this acceptance in several different ways.

Show OH 139, Three Basic Ways to Create an Environment of Acceptance.

Pictures and Posters

Ask how many teachers display pictures and posters in their classrooms. Comment that the pictures a teacher displays create a child's first impression of the classroom environment. Discuss each item on overheads 140a and 140b and how each contributes to an accepting environment.

Show OH 140a and **140b,** Classroom Pictures Should Include.

Books

Say that the Spark books were chosen partly because they show diverse people in diverse environments. Display the following books from Spark as examples.

People of different color and race:

Abiyoyo—Say that it is all right to have books that show people of only one race as long as there are a variety of books covering a variety of races in the classroom. Tell them to be sure to tell the children that the people in the *Abiyoyo* illustrations are dressed in traditional clothing, not dressed as they would be today.

Show *Abiyoyo* crowd pictures.

Males and females in nonstereotypical roles and professions:

Mama, Do You Love Me?—Show the cover of this book and say that the mother is shown as a capable woman, paddling the umiak. Then turn to the title page and explain that it is all right to show characters in traditional roles, such as the mother sewing, as long as there is a balance of roles in the entire classroom book collection.

Show *Mama, Do You Love Me?* woman in atypical role, then in typical role.

People with disabilities in active roles:

No Fair to Tigers—Show any of the illustrations that show Mandy in her wheelchair. Say that it is okay if a book does not make direct reference to the diversity being shown. In this book, the fact that the child is in a wheelchair is not the focus of the story until she encounters a situation that is unfair to people who use wheelchairs. It is valuable for children to see people with disabilities take an active role with other characters in the general action of the story.

Show *No Fair to Tigers;* describe role of disability in the story.

People of different ages in capable roles:

The Napping House—Show the picture (near the end of the book) of Granny and the other characters falling off the broken

Show *The Napping House,* example of elderly, active character.

bed. Say that in this book Granny is depicted as an active, capable person.

Different types of homes, cultures, and lifestyles:

Show *Jonathan and His Mommy; I Need a Lunch Box; Baby Rattlesnake; Tree of Cranes; Mama, Do You Love Me?* and *No Fair to Tigers.* Explain that all these books show people who are different from one another, and that the collection of books in a classroom should reflect all the kinds of human differences that were listed on the transparency, and any others they can think of. The Spark curriculum deliberately uses books that show a wide range of diversity.

Say that it is also important to be sure that the classroom includes books in which a female is the main character, using *Mama, Do You Love Me?* as an example.

Show books and discuss cultural and family differences.

Show *Mama, Do You Love Me?* as example of female main character.

Music

State that music is an area in which openness to other cultures can easily be encouraged. Research indicates that young children are open to all types of music. For this reason, it is important to include music from other cultures and music in many styles in the curriculum. Say that the Spark curriculum suggests including many types and styles of music, including music from other countries and classical, folk, popular, Dixieland, jazz, and blues. If you plan to present the music workshop, say that the music used in the curriculum will be discussed in greater detail during the music and movement workshop that is a part of this training.

Talk about diversity in music; note separate music center workshop later in training.

The Activities in the Classroom

The Spark center activities are open-ended and therefore allow for a wide variety of individual responses to materials. There are two types of activities that occur regularly in Spark that allow children to explore and share their own cultural experiences: story time and make-believe play.

Show *Mama, Do You Love Me?* and remind participants that whenever teachers read a story, they are encouraged to include discussion. The discussion should include questions that encourage children to share their own real-life experiences.

Say that one question a teacher might ask after showing children the cover of this book is "The mother and the child are riding in a boat. What kinds of things do you ride in?"

Say that this question is an early lesson in social studies, as children compare their own means of transportation to those of

Talk about open-ended activities and cultural experience.

Show *Mama, Do You Love Me?* Talk about children's experience.

Model using a question to encourage discussion.

Refer to question as "social studies."

people in a different culture. As children listen to each other's responses, they also compare their own means of transportation to those of others in the classroom in an accepting way. For example, some children might primarily ride in a car, while others often ride in a bus, truck, or taxi.

Ask participants to suggest other questions about this picture they might ask that encourage children to share their own experiences. Questions might include "Did you ever ride in a boat?" "What did it look like?" "What made it move?" "What are the mother and child wearing?" "Do you wear clothes like theirs?" "What do you wear when you go outside?"

Say that by sharing their experiences, children find out that everyone does not live exactly the same way. When teachers respond in a positive way to the children's responses, they give the message that it's a normal and positive aspect of life that everyone's life experiences are unique. Help children to identify both the things they have in common with other people, such as someone who loves them, and the things that may be different, such as the way they dress or their homes.

Responding to Children

State that the Spark curriculum has been designed to promote learning in children from many different backgrounds and of widely differing skill levels. The open-ended center activities offer opportunities for children to make choices of how they use the materials. Children are encouraged to choose center activities that best fit their personal preferences. Throughout the Spark hour, children are encouraged to enter into discussions and share experiences.

Fitting Spark into the Lesson Plan

Say that the overhead shows a suggested plan for the day's activities when Spark is used in the classroom. Discuss the schedule with the participants, allowing time for discussion and suggestions for adapting according to needs. After teachers become familiar with the Spark Curriculum and the teaching strategies, they may adapt it in many ways to fit their individual program and to meet the needs of individual children.

Say that teachers have adapted Spark to suit their needs in many ways. Some have used music and movement activities with large groups, either in the gymnasium or in the classroom. Others have spread one unit over two weeks in order to use more of

Ask participants to suggest questions.

Show OH 141 Sample Spark Classroom Schedule.

Show OH 142, Adaptations (Teacher Suggestions).

Show OH 143a and 143b, What Stories Can I Put Together for a Theme?

the center activities. These teachers varied story time by telling the story the second week or by using flannelboard figures.

A project approach can also be used by introducing a Spark unit and then expanding it into other projects. Two examples are a spider unit based on *Anansi and the Moss-Covered Rock* and an insect unit based on *The Very Quiet Cricket.* Say that supplemental books may also be used to expand the unit for a second week. Say that they will find a resource list in the front of their first acivity book.

Say that some programs like to have month-long units based on a central theme. Suggestions for central themes might include units based on the books listed on the overheads.

Summary

Show OH 144, To Promote Growth through Literacy and the Arts.

Ask what the purpose of the Spark curriculum is. Encourage discussion and then display overhead 144. State that the Spark activities are merely activities based on the creative arts that are to be used as a vehicle to promote children's skills.

Tell the participants that you talked earlier about what the parts of the daily units were.

Review the child and teacher behaviors that are encouraged. If necessary, show overheads 127, 128, and 129a and b.

Show OH 145a and 145b, Summary.

Draw the participants' attention to the handout titled Implementing the Spark Curriculum. Tell them to use this handout as a reference as they begin to implement the curriculum. Show overheads 145a and 145b, and tell them that these review the points they've learned during today's training. Review the points on the overhead one at a time; allow for discussion.

Show **OH 146,** Teacher Comments.

Remind them that they've covered a lot of information in the workshop. Show overhead 146 and say that although it may seem overwhelming at first, the Spark curriculum will make their jobs easier and their time with the children more enjoyable, as well as developing the children's skills.

Thank everyone for their attention and contributions to the discussions. If appropriate, tell them that the next workshop(s) will introduce them to the arts activities. Tell them to dress casually because they will be on the floor, moving to music, and may even be painting.

SPARK STORIES

Name of Story	Ethnicity of Story	Gender of Main Character	Concepts
Abiyoyo	African	Male	Disappear Shadows Faster Happy
Anansi and the Moss-Covered Rock	African	Male (Spider)	Covered Behind/In Front Of Spiders All
Baby Rattlesnake	Native American	Male (Snake)	Family Shake Closer Snakes
Big Al	European-American	Male (Fish)	Ocean Making Friends Same/Different Strong
The Bossy Gallito	Cuban	Male (Rooster)	Rooster Please/Thank You Dirty/Clean Hurry

Name of Story	Ethnicity of Story	Gender of Main Character	Concepts
Chicka Chicka Boom Boom	European-American	Either (Letters)	Top/Bottom Enough Family Coconut
I Need a Lunch Box	African-American	Male	In Colors Rectangle Parade
If You Give a Pig a Pancake	European-American	Female	Pancakes Sticky Homesick Under
Jamela's Dress	South African	Female	Patterns Special Fold Feelings
Jonathan and His Mommy	African-American	Male	Giant/Tiny Backward Twirling City

Name of Story	Ethnicity of Story	Gender of Main Character	Concepts
The Lady with the Alligator Purse	European-American	Female	In/Out Eating Telephone Talk Helping Sick People
The Little Mouse, the Red Ripe Strawberry, and the Big Hungry Bear	English	Either (Mouse)	Senses Colors Half Share
Mama, Do You Love Me?	Native American, Inuit	Female	People Who Love One Another Large/Small Cold Feelings
The Napping House	English	Both	On/Off Falling Down Counting Happy
Nine-in-One Grr! Grr!	Laos, Hmong	Female	Tigers How Many Remember Same/Different

Name of Story	Ethnicity of Story	Gender of Main Character	Concepts
No Fair to Tigers	European-American	Female	Orange, Black, White Fair/No Fair Ramp/Stairs Wheels
Polar Bear, Polar Bear, What Do You Hear?	European-American	Either (Animals)	Animal Sounds Sounds Around Us Listening (2 days)
The Snowy Day	African-American	Male	Snow Covered Melt Making a Story
Tree of Cranes	Japanese	Male	Feelings Hot/Cold Open/Close Quiet
The Very Quiet Cricket	European-American	Male (Cricket)	Rubbing Big/Little Together Insects

Abiyoyo

Day	Concept	Music Activity	Art Activity	Make-Believe Activity
Day 1	Disappear (Cognitive, Science)	Make sounds disappear by holding hand over mouth, turning off tape recorder, and stopping vibrations of instruments.	Paint with water, product disappears as it dries.	Pretend to be magician. Make bubbles disappear by touching them with wand.
Day 2	Shadows (Cognitive, Science)	Make dancing shadows by moving to music before strong light (streamers).	Make junk structures that cast shadows.	Toy figures make shadows (flashlights).
Day 3	Faster (Cognitive, Language)	Sing, move to drumbeat, move and play instruments faster to a drumbeat.	Fingerpaint faster to a recited rhyme. Mix blue and green paint, make circles with a craft stick.	Race toy vehicles on ramps to determine which one is faster.
Day 4	Happy (Social)	Sing happy songs, move or play instruments to "happy" music.	Make a happy collage by cutting out magazine pictures and gluing them and other items such as sequins, glitter.	Pretend to be clowns (face paint).
Day 5	The Circus			

Anansi and the Moss-Covered Rock

Day	Concept	Music Activity	Art Activity	Make-Believe Activity
Day 1	Covered (Cognitive, Language)	Cover and uncover instruments, comparing sounds.	Cover (glue and paint mixture) rocks and boxes with assorted materials.	Take turns being the moss-covered rock.
Day 2	Behind/ In Front Of (Cognitive, Language, Motor)	Play "follow the leader" moving behind and in front of objects.	Make a puppet stage, stand behind and in front of it with puppets.	Combine with art center.
Day 3	Spiders (Cognitive, Science)	Walk around a masking tape "web" on the floor to "spider" music.	Sponge paint over a cutout of a spider to make a spider print on paper.	Pretend to be a spider. Take a nature walk to look for spiders.
Day 4	All (Cognitive, Language, Math)	Gather all the play food to song. Gather shapes to song.	Child picks an object out of tub, puts it in sack, then glues all the objects onto a surface.	Make fruit salad from all the fruit.
Day 5	Puppet Show			

Big Al

Day	Concept	Music Activity	Art Activity	Make-Believe Activity
Day 1	Ocean (Cognitive, Language, Science)	Pretend to play at the shore. Move to music.	Fingerpaint with salt and paint.	Color water blue. Water table play.
Day 2	Making Friends (Language, Social)	Play and share instruments with friends.	Paint a pretend boat together.	Wrap self in seaweed and swim around the room.
Day 3	Same/ Different (Cognitive, Language)	Play "Simon Says" game to Big Al chant.	Cut various items and make a picture.	Fish with fishing poles.
Day 4	Strong (Cognitive, Language, Science)	Identify pictures of strong animals; move like them.	Make a sculpture out of materials that are strong.	Collect strong objects on a nature walk.
Day 5	A Day at the Beach			

The Bossy Gallito

Day	Concept	Music Activity	Art Activity	Make-Believe Activity
Day 1	Rooster (Cognitive, Language)	Identify farm animals by sound and move like roosters to the Bossy Gallito song.	Paint with feather dusters.	Build homes for chickens with blocks.
Day 2	Please/ Thank You (Social)	Use target terms to obtain instruments to play to Cuban music in a pretend wedding band.	Use target terms as materials are shared. (Markers to decorate communal box.)	Use target terms at pretend fast food restaurant.
Day 3	Dirty/Clean (Cognitive, Language, Social)	Get fingers dirty in flour, clean by participating in "Hokey Pokey" game.	Fingerpaint on table, then clean it off.	Wash toy dishes.
Day 4	Hurry (Cognitive, Language, Motor)	Move like roosters in various ways as they hurry to fast music.	Hurry as they make prints on paper with three-dimensional objects.	Hurry as they pretend to be firefighters.
Day 5	Building a Farm			

ACTIVITY MATRIX

The Little Mouse, the Red Ripe Strawberry, and the Big Hungry Bear

Day	Concept	Music Activity	Art Activity	Make-Believe Activity
Day 1	Senses: Hear, See, Smell (Science)	(Hear) Compare sounds and movements of the bear and the mouse.	(See) Look through the book together. List what they see. Provide a variety of materials to enable them to make whatever they choose.	(Smell) Children pretend to be the Big Hungry Bear and try to find an object by using their sense of smell.
Day 2	Colors (Cognitive, Kindergarten Readiness)	Play recorded music as children march around color shapes. When the music stops, sit on the nearest shape. Sing color song.	Mix paint in resealable plastic bags. Discuss resulting colors and paint freely with the paint.	Use play food of different colors. Pretend to be mouse and bear preparing dinner.
Day 3	Half (Math)	Divide the children into 2 equal groups. Count children, stressing half. Children play instruments loudly with bear music and quietly with mouse music.	Make art prints with halves of vegetables dipped in thick paint.	Children cut paper fruit in half, then share their fruit with a stuffed animal friend.
Day 4	Share (Social)	Pass an instrument around circle, singing the Share Song to the tune of "Mary Had a Little Lamb."	Children make Styrofoam structure to use as a hiding place for the strawberry. Limited supplies to share.	Share food supplies to make individual snacks.
Day 5	Strawberries (Nutrition activity)			

Tree of Cranes

Day	Concept	Music Activity	Art Activity	Make-Believe Activity
Day 1	Feelings (Social)	Play musical instruments and decide how the sounds make them feel.	Make a mural of things that make them smile and things that make them frown.	Actions that others are pretending to do, and the feelings that they are pretending to feel.
Day 2	Hot/Cold (Cognitive, Language, Science)	Investigate cold and hot sounds by playing ice drums, swishing ice strikers through warm water, and walking in ice boots.	Uses ice cubes and warm water in sand play.	Pretend to prepare hot and cold foods.
Day 3	Open/Close (Cognitive, Language)	Experiment with a jingle bell in an open and closed bag.	Put playdough and food coloring in plastic bags and mix them together.	Prepare pretend gifts to give away.
Day 4	Quiet (Cognitive, Language)	Play bells quietly. Play a quiet music game.	Use quiet materials for making sculptures.	Create a quiet place for doing quiet things.
Day 5	Decorating Trees			

The Very Quiet Cricket

Day	Concept	Music Activity	Art Activity	Make-Believe Activity
Day 1	Rubbing (Cognitive, Language, Motor)	Different musical instruments to determine which ones can be played by rubbing them.	Make crayon or chalk rubbings.	Rub table with sponge to get it clean for a pretend birthday party.
Day 2	Big/Little (Cognitive, Language, Social)	Discriminate big and little shapes as they play the "Hokey Pokey."	Make big and little items with playdough.	Pretend to be adults taking care of babies.
Day 3	Together (Cognitive, Language, Social)	Move to music together. Do mirror movements.	Mix ingredients for fingerpaint.	Rub fabrics together and pretend to wash doll clothes.
Day 4	Insects (Cognitive, Language, Science)	Use kazoos to sound like insects and streamers to "fly" like insects.	Make insects from boxes, Styrofoam balls, and other materials.	Make pretend insect homes and pretend to be insects.
Day 5	Insect World			

Abiyoyo
Day 1: Art Center

What to Do:

This activity is most successful when it is done outdoors; however, it may also be done indoors on a chalkboard. You may need a fan to make the chalkboard dry quickly.

Relate the activity to the story. Sit with the children to discuss the activity before you start. Remind them that in the story, the father made things disappear. Say that they are going to paint and their paintings will disappear.

Take the materials outside to a sidewalk. If the weather permits, take the children, a bucket of water, brushes, rollers, sponges, and small containers outside to where there is a sidewalk.

"Paint" on the sidewalk. Give each child a small container full of water and a brush, roller, or sponge. Join the children in painting circles, squares, large lines, small lines, and other shapes with water on the sidewalk. Encourage them to work together. Discuss the marks they make with the different equipment: What type of mark did you make with the roller? What kinds of marks can you make with the sponge? Encourage older children to make drawings of people.

"Paint" on another place on the sidewalk. After a short time, have everyone move down the sidewalk to another place to make another group painting.

See if the first painting has disappeared. Go back to the first artwork to see if it is still visible. Has it disappeared? What made it disappear?

Anansi and the Moss-Covered Rock
Day 1: Art Center

What to Do:

Relate the activity to the story. Remind the children that Anansi the Spider found a magic moss-covered rock. Say that they are going to make their own covered rocks, but that their rocks might be glitter-covered rocks, or cloth-covered rocks. They may cover their rocks with different things.

Cover the rocks with paint. Demonstrate painting a rock, as you encourage the children to cover their own rocks with paint. As everyone paints, prompt discussion about how shiny the paint looks, the color of the paint mixture, and how the children are making the rocks look like moss-covered rocks. When they are finished, put them aside to dry.

Cover boxes and rocks with different materials. Put out the boxes and unpainted rocks, the glue, and the materials for covering the boxes. Invite the children to cover their boxes and rocks with any of the materials they wish to use. Join in and model covering a rock or a box completely. Ask the children to describe their decorated rocks or boxes ("a cotton-covered box," or "a rock covered with paper and glitter").

Change the covered table into a clean one. When the children are finished, remark that the table is covered with many things. Have the children name all the things on the table. Then ask them to change the covered table into a clean one.

MATERIALS

- Rocks, two or more for each child and each adult
- Paintbrushes
- Paint mixture (combine 2 tablespoons liquid starch, 2 tablespoons water, 1 tablespoon green paint powder or food coloring, and ½ cup salt)
- Small boxes, one or more for each child and each adult
- Glue
- Materials for covering rocks and boxes, such as cotton balls, sand, glitter, Styrofoam chips, tissue paper, shiny paper, wrapping paper, newspaper, scraps of cloth

Big Al
Day 1: Art Center

What to Do:

Relate the activity to the story. Remind the children that the water where Big Al lived was very salty. They will make salty fingerpaint pictures.

Fingerpaint with salt and paint. Place containers of salt and fingerpaint on the table. Remind the children that Big Al lived in the ocean and that ocean water is salty water. Encourage the children to add salt to the fingerpaint, then use the paint to make swirly designs on the paper like moving water.

Discuss texture, designs. Ask the children how the paint feels without the salt. How does it feel after they add salt? Is it still smooth? Discuss the marks they made on their paper. Do their marks look like waves? How could they make them look more like waves?

Trace around fish shapes. Place the fish shapes and craft sticks on the table. Say that you are going to put fish in your ocean. Trace around the fish shapes with a craft stick or your finger. Encourage the children to trace fish shapes on their papers.

Discuss the fish shapes. Ask the children how many fish are in their oceans. Do some of their fish look the same? Are their fish big or little? Is one of their fish Big Al?

MATERIALS

- Fingerpaint
- Containers of salt
- Paper for fingerpainting
- Fish shapes of different sizes (large for young children, gradually smaller for older children)
- Craft sticks

Big Al
Day 2: Art Center

What to Do:

Relate the activity to the story. Remind the children that Big Al wanted to be friends with the other fish. He tried very hard to make friends. Say that one thing some people do with their friends is to go boating together. Say that they are going to make a boat and that they will all work together as they paint and decorate the boat. Suggest that another way to make friends is to do things together and share materials.

Paint a large box together. Provide a variety of paint, brushes, pieces of decorative papers, glue, and markers. Work with the children to paint and decorate the boat. Encourage the children to discuss experiences they may have had with boats as they work. Ask them if they have ever been in a boat. What kind of boat was it? Who were they with? Did they go fishing?

Encourage working together and sharing. As you work with the children emphasize that everyone is working together and sharing materials with their friends. Encourage children to ask one another for materials and praise children who share.

Name the boat. Tell the children that boats often have names. Ask them to suggest a name for their boat. Paint the name on the boat.

Save the boat. Save the boat for day 3 make-believe and day 5 large-group activities.

MATERIALS

■ Rectangular box, preferably large enough for two children to sit in

■ Paint

■ Paintbrushes

■ Markers

■ Decorative strips of paper

■ Glue

The Bossy Gallito
Day 3: Music and Movement Center

What to Do:

Relate the activity to the story. Remind the children that when the little rooster ate the corn he got his beak dirty and that grass finally helped him get clean again. Say that they're going to play a music game. They will pretend that they are dirty and then will get clean.

Sit with the children in a circle on the floor. Place the container of water in the middle of the circle. Encourage each child to put his finger in the container of flour. Then, with the children still seated, sing the "Hokey Pokey" song, using the following words. As you sing, show how you put your finger in the water, encouraging the children to join you. Repeat using thumb, other fingers, elbow, and so on.

> *You put your finger in.*
> *You take your finger out.*
> *You put your finger in and you swish it all around.*
> *You do the Hokey Pokey and you wave it all around.*
> *That's what it's all about!*

Encourage the children to look at their fingers. Are they clean? Give each child a paper towel, encouraging them to say *thank you.* Have them wipe their fingers off with the paper towels, as the grass wiped the Bossy Gallito's beak.

Have the children stand to continue the game. (Remove the container of water.) Ask the children to please stand up, remaining in the circle. Thank them. Tell them that you are pretending that the middle of the circle is a great big container of water like a bathtub and that they will pretend to put parts of their body in the water as they do what the song tells them to do. Sing the "Hokey Pokey" and model the actions, encouraging the children to follow your lead. Start with large body parts such as arms and legs, then move on to body parts that the children need to learn to identify such as elbow, finger, or nose. (Ask older children for suggestions.)

End the activity by singing the Bossy Gallito song from day 1. Have the children sit down. Sing the Bossy Gallito song quietly, encouraging them to sing or move to the song, and crow.

MATERIALS
- Large container of water
- Small container of flour
- Paper towels, one for each child and each adult

The Little Mouse, the Red Ripe Strawberry, and the Big Hungry Bear

Day 3: Music and Movement Center

What to Do:

This activity works best when there are an even number of children.

Relate the activity to the story. Remind the children that the mouse divided the strawberry in half, then gave half of it away and ate the other half.

Divide the group of children in half. Tell the children to stand up. Have them help you count them, then say you need ____ to be bears and ____ to be mice. Ask the bears to sit on one side of you and the mice to sit on the other side. Say that the group is divided in half.

Choose instruments to play. Place the instruments where the children can reach them easily, then encourage them to choose an instrument to play. Ask them if the bears should play loud instruments or quiet ones. Ask if mice should play loud instruments or quiet ones.

Play sections of the music and encourage the children to play their instruments. Encourage them to play loudly with the "bear" music and quietly with the "mouse" music.

Play music again, for the children to move. Have the children change roles, with the mice becoming bears and the bears becoming mice. Let the children choose whether they want to move to the music or play an instrument. Some children may be able to do both.

Sing the Big Hungry Bear song to the tune of "Twinkle, Twinkle, Little Star."

> The <u>big</u> hungry <u>bear</u> tromps <u>through</u> the forest <u>green</u>
> <u>Sniff</u>ing for a <u>ber</u>ry that <u>he</u> can't <u>see</u>
> <u>Tromp,</u> tromp, <u>tromp</u> go his <u>big</u> bear <u>feet</u>
> <u>Tromp,</u> tromp, <u>tromp</u> go his <u>big</u> bear <u>feet</u>
> The <u>big</u> hungry <u>bear</u> tromps <u>through</u> the forest <u>green</u>
> <u>Sniff</u>ing for a <u>ber</u>ry that <u>he</u> can't <u>see!</u>
>
> The <u>hung</u>ry <u>mouse</u> sneaks <u>through</u> the forest <u>green</u>
> <u>Hid</u>ing the <u>ber</u>ry so the <u>bear</u> can't <u>see</u>
> <u>Sneak,</u> sneak, <u>sneak</u> go her <u>lit</u>tle mouse <u>feet</u>
> <u>Sneak,</u> sneak, <u>sneak</u> go her <u>lit</u>tle mouse <u>feet</u>
> The <u>hung</u>ry <u>mouse</u> sneaks through the forest <u>green</u>
> <u>Hid</u>ing the <u>ber</u>ry so the <u>bear</u> can't <u>see!</u>

The Little Mouse, the Red Ripe Strawberry, and the Big Hungry Bear

Day 3: Make-Believe Center

What to Do:

If the group includes children who cannot cut, cut some of the paper fruit in half before the activity begins.

Relate the activity to the story. Remind the children that the mouse cut the strawberry in half and shared it with his friend. Say that they will cut a piece of paper fruit in half, then share it with a pretend friend.

Cut the paper fruit in half. Place the fruit and scissors in the center of the table where they are easily available and encourage each child to take a fruit shape and a pair of scissors. Ask each child to label his fruit and its color. Give help as needed as they cut their fruit in half.

Encourage children to choose a stuffed animal friend. Ask the children who the mouse's friend was in the story. Say that they can pretend that the stuffed animal is the friend with whom they share their fruit. Encourage them to use any of the housekeeping materials, blocks, or whatever they wish to create an environment in which they may share their strawberry with their friend. (For example, they may wish to make a block chair for their friend, or create a box table to place dishes on.)

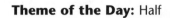

MATERIALS

- Pieces of paper fruit with a heavy black line drawn down the center (strawberries, bananas, oranges, apples, etc.)
- Scissors (enough for each child to have a pair)
- Stuffed animals, enough for each child to have one
- Blocks, empty boxes, dishes

Tree of Cranes
Day 2: Music and Movement Center

What to Do:

Relate the activity to the story. Ask the children what the boy did to get his mittens wet. Ask if they have ever played in cold water. If appropriate, encourage them to share their experiences by asking if adults got angry when they played in cold water. Say that they will make sounds with very cold things in this activity!

Strike cans with the ice strikers. Distribute the ice strikers and cans. Play the "ice drums," with the children and show how to gently hit the strikers together like rhythm sticks and gently hit the can with them. Discuss how cold the strikers are and ask what happens to the strikers as the children hold and play them. (They're melting.) If the children know the song "Jingle Bells," encourage them to sing the song as they tap their cans.

Experiment with warm water. Encourage the children to swish their ice strikers around in the warm water, listen to the sounds and discover what happens when ice is in warm water. Encourage them to discuss what is happening to the ice. If you live in an area of the country where winter brings snow and ice, compare their ice to the icicles that form when snow melts and refreezes.

Walk around in frozen plastic bags. Distribute the frozen bags and encourage the children to put them over their shoes. Talk about the sounds made by the cold bags as the children handle them. Encourage the children to walk around in the bags, making sounds with their feet. As the bags get warm, discuss how the sound is changing.

Sing a song. Show the children page 32 in the book, drawing their attention to the snowman. Ask if they think the snowman is hot or cold. Sing the following words to the tune of "I'm a Little Teapot":

> *I'm a little snowman, I'm so cold,*
> *I'm made of snow and chunks of coal.*
> *Put a big hat and scarf on me,*
> *I'll make you happy when you see me.*

MATERIALS

- Ice strikers, enough for each child and each adult to have two (see Day 2: Group Time)
- Empty tin cans, enough for each child and each adult to have one
- Frozen plastic bags to go over children's shoes
- Container of warm water
- Book, *Tree of Cranes*

The Very Quiet Cricket
Day 1: Art Center

What to Do:

Relate the activity to the story. Ask the children what crickets do to make a sound. Do crickets talk like we do? Do crickets bark like dogs, meow like cats? Say that they will rub things to make pictures the way the cricket rubbed his wings together to make a sound.

Show how to use the materials. Place the materials where they are easily accessible. If you are using crayons, explain that it is easier to rub crayons on paper if they are peeled. Show how to peel a crayon; let each child choose a crayon to use and peel it, telling its color. When each child has a peeled crayon or piece of chalk, ask them each to get a piece of paper and choose something flat to put under it from the assortment of objects you have gathered.

Make rubbings. Place an object under your piece of paper and show the children how to make a rubbing. To help anchor the paper as the child rubs, tape the corners of the paper to the table. Show how to rub the crayon or chalk hard over the object so that the impression shows up clearly. Emphasize the word "rub" as the children work. Let them make rubbings of several things, and suggest that they trade crayons or chalk with each other, so that each rubbing has several different colors.

Label objects in the rubbings. When the children have made rubbings of a few objects, ask everyone to stop to look at the papers. Tell them to try to identify the objects in each other's rubbings. They might also match the real objects to the impressions in the rubbings.

Paint over the rubbings. To extend the activity, let the children paint over the crayon rubbings with watery paint. The crayon markings will resist the paint. (Chalk rubbings will not resist the paint.)

MATERIALS

- Crayons or colored sidewalk chalk
- White paper
- Flat, textured objects to place under paper, such as doilies, geometric shapes, cutouts of letters of the alphabet, keys, paper clips, combs
- Transparent or masking tape
- Watery paint and brushes (optional)

The Very Quiet Cricket
Day 3: Make-Believe Center

What to Do:

Relate the activity to the story. Say that the cricket had to rub his wings together to make a sound. Remind them that on another day, they rubbed the table to get it clean. Now they are going to rub clothes together to make them clean.

Mix soap and water. Have the children stand around the water table or give each child a bowl of water. Let them squirt soap in the water, telling them how many times to squeeze the bottle.

Wash the clothes. Give each child at least two pieces of clothing or other fabric items to wash in the water. Prompt them to rub the items together to get the dirt out.

Wring water out of the clothes. After they have washed for a while, demonstrate swishing the clothes around in the water, squeezing them, and twisting them to get the water out.

Hang clothes to dry. Show the children how to hang the clothes on the clothesline and attach the clothespins, encouraging them to use a pincer grasp to squeeze the clothespins. As the children work, discuss how adults wash and dry clothes at their homes, and how it compares to what they are doing.

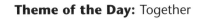

MATERIALS

- Water table or one bowl of warm water per child
- Bottles of liquid soap
- Doll clothes or other small fabric items
- Clothesline or heavy string suspended between two chairs
- Spring-type clothespins

Teaching through the Activity

1. What skills can I help children develop during this activity? (Please check all that can be addressed.) How?

       o Vocabulary/Language
       o Readiness skills such as colors, shapes, etc.
       o Fine Motor
       o Gross Motor
       o Social

_____

_____

_____

2. How can I change the activity to fit the special needs of an individual child? (Use the child assigned to your group.)

_____

_____

_____

_____

_____

3. What other experience areas can be related to this activity? (Please check all that apply.) How?

       o Science
       o Nutrition
       o Math
       o Writing (pre-literacy)
       o Music
       o Art
       o Sensory

_____

_____

_____

Implementing the Spark Curriculum

To prepare:

- Read through the unit.

- Read through the day's activities.

- Read through the story and deciding how to make it interesting.

- Decide which child goals to address during the day's activities.

- Learn songs and/or raps.

- Listen to music.

- Gather all needed materials.

During Spark Time:

- Allow approximately an hour for Spark at least four days a week.

- Group Activity: (The group activity typically lasts between fifteen and thirty minutes). The length of the activity will depend upon the activity and the day in the sequence. For example, the first day a unit is introduced, the group activity is typically shorter, because there is no review of a previous day's activities.

  - During the reading of the story, enable children to become involved by asking them questions and encouraging them to become physically (make gestures with hands) and verbally (repeat phrases) involved.

  - During the group activity, encourage children to choose the first activity they will attend.

- Center Activities: The time varies depending upon the activity and the skill level of the children. Most will last approximately fifteen minutes. After the children finish with the first center, they usually move to the other center; therefore, each of the center activities needs to be repeated to give each child a chance to participate.

  - During the center activities, encourage children to choose both materials (such as colors of markers, paints, crayons, instruments, dress-up clothes) and how they wish to use the materials (encourage children to be creative).

- Stress the concept of the day throughout the activities. After the day the concept is introduced, continue to stress the concept whenever it is appropriate to do so.

- Provide positive reinforcement throughout the day's activities.

- Ask both closed questions (a definite answer is expected, for example, "What color is the circle?") and open-ended questions ("What could the boy do outside in the snow?").

- Encourage problem solving.

- Teach by being actively involved in the activity. Use a combination of direct teaching and modeling.

Goals of the Spark Workshop

- To become familiar with the components of the Spark curriculum

- To become familiar with the curriculum format and activities

- To gain understanding of suggested strategies

- To understand how Spark helps create an inclusive environment

Goals of Spark

Use creative arts and literacy activities as vehicles to

- Promote general-readiness skills.

- Promote individual skills.

- Expand children's store of knowledge.

- Get families involved in the learning process.

Premise

Preschool children's goals can be promoted through a curriculum based on literacy and the creative arts.

Components of the Spark Curriculum

- The Creative Arts Curriculum

- In-service Training

- Family Involvement

Characteristics of Spark Activities

- Teachers introduce activities, then children engage in experiential learning.

- A combination of direct teaching and modeling is encouraged.

- Teachers use discussion, physical actions, chants, and songs to encourage child involvement.

- Child choice is encouraged.

Characteristics of Spark Activities (Continued)

- Activities are related to stories and the theme of the day in order to make them meaningful.

- Activities offer multisensory experiences, thus encouraging generalization of skills.

- Teachers are expected to be active participants in activities.

Cultural Diversity

Stories:

- African
- African-American
- Cuban

- European-American
- Hmong
- Inuit

- Japanese
- Native-American

Family Materials

STORY OF THE WEEK / EL CUENTO DE ESTA SEMANA

Abiyoyo
by Pete Seeger

The Spark story this week is *Abiyoyo*, based on a folktale from South Africa. You may be able to find this book or an audiotape of the story at the library. The story is about a monster named Abiyoyo who comes to the village where a little boy lives with his father. Everyone is scared because they think the monster will eat them alive. The little boy and his father are very brave. The little boy plays his ukulele and sings a song about the monster. Abiyoyo starts to dance. When Abiyoyo falls down, the father makes Abiyoyo disappear! Ask your child to sing the Abiyoyo song to you and show you how Abiyoyo danced faster and faster until he fell down. Ask your child what Abiyoyo ate (whole cows and sheep!). The themes to go with this story are *disappear, shadows, faster,* and *happy.*

El cuento de Spark de esta semana se llama *Abiyoyo* y está basado en un cuento folklórico sudafricano. Puedes encontrar tanto el libro como el *audiotape* del cuento, en inglés, en cualquier biblioteca. Un día un monstruo llamado Abiyoyo llegó a un pueblo, adonde un niño pequeño vivía con su padre. Mientras todos se asustaron pensando que el monstruo los iba a comer vivos, el niñito y su padre fueron muy valientes. ¡El muchachito hasta tocó el ukelele y cantó una canción sobre el monstruo! Abiyoyo, el monstruo, comenzó a bailar. Luego se cayó y el padre del niñito hizo que desapareciera. Pídale a su niño o niña que le cante la canción de Abiyoyo y que le muestre cómo Abiyoyo bailaba, cada vez más rápido hasta que se cayó. Pregúntele a su niño o niña qué comía Abiyoyo (¡vacas y ovejas enteras!). Las palabras temáticas son: *desaparecer, sombras, más rápido y feliz.*

The Spark Curriculum

The Spark Creative Arts Curriculum is a culturally sensitive preschool curriculum, based on children's literature, that enables the children to learn individual and general early childhood skills through the creative arts.

The Spark Curriculum

has two major parts:

- Story time (large group)

- Center activities (small groups)

Abiyoyo Matrix

Day 1: Disappear

- Music: Make sounds disappear

- Art: Paint with water

- Make-Believe: Make bubbles disappear

Day 2: Shadows

- Music: Make dancing shadows

- Art: Make junk structures that cast shadows

- Make-Believe: Make shadows with toy figures

Day 3: Faster

- Music: Sing, move, play instruments faster

- Art: Fingerpaint faster to rhyme

- Make-Believe: Race toy vehicles to decide which is faster

Embedded Teaching Strategies

- Story is repeated daily

- Ethnic stories/music used

- New skills are modeled before children choose centers

- Unifying theme used throughout the Spark hour

- Child physical/verbal involvement encouraged during story reading

Spark Unit Organization

- Introduction

- Activity Matrix

- Activities

- Skills Promoted

- Family Handout

Story Descriptions

Abiyoyo
by Pete Seeger
New York: Macmillan, 1986.

Story Synopsis: The African folktale "Abiyoyo" takes place in a small village. It centers on a boy and his father and their encounters with Abiyoyo, a giant. The story is intriguing to children because the giant who terrorizes the village is made to disappear through the efforts of the boy and his father.

Classroom Use: The Abiyoyo unit has proved to be a favorite with children in preschool classrooms. Teachers report that "this unit is our all-time favorite" and that "*disappear* has become a part of the children's vocabulary." The story is appropriate for any season; however, it is longer than many stories read to young children and contains some unfamiliar words, such as *ostracize* and *disappear*. Even though the story is longer and more complex than many preschool stories, many teachers link it to their Halloween theme. It may be grouped with units based on monster stories, African stories, or families. The themes and concepts on which the daily activities are based are *disappear, shadows, faster,* and *happy.*

Considerations: The illustrations contain stereotypical pictures of people from different cultures. If you use this unit, you may want to discuss the fact that the story is based on a folktale, and the fact that the pictures show people in their traditional dress, not in the contemporary clothing they wear now.

Special Materials: Most of the materials used for this unit are typically found in early childhood classrooms. The first day's activities suggest the use of bubble solution.

18

Spark Activity Format, Day 1

Story/Large Group (20 minutes)

- Read story

- Introduce focus concept

- Introduce center activities

Center Activities (20 minutes)

- Music and Movement

- Art

- Make-Believe

Introducing Center Activities

- Let's make them enticing!

- Don't just tell the children about it; model what will happen.

The Importance of Center Introduction

Introductions

- Enable children to make informed choices.

- Enable the teacher to teach new skills.

- Relate the center activity to the story.

The Purpose of Center Activity

- Promote children's general and individual skills.

- Reinforce the concept of the day.

Spark Center Activities

- Music and Movement Activities

- Art Activities

- Make-Believe Activities

Using Arts Activities

- Music and movement, art, and make-believe all have different attributes.

- Each area promotes skills in different ways and to different degrees.

Spark Format, Days 2, 3, 4

- Review previous day's activities.

- Read story and discuss.

- Introduce theme of the day.

- Introduce centers.

- Teach through center activities.

Review of Center Activities

Activities:

- Reinforce concept.

- Provide continuity.

- Promote conversational language.

- Promote memory skills.

- Provide opportunity to promote general and individual skills.

Spark Format, Day 5

- Create make-believe setting

- Review concepts from days 1–4

Process over Product

- Specific products do not meet individual children's needs.

- Product activities cause children frustration and feelings of failure.

Teacher's Role during Center Activities

- To facilitate general learning.

- To promote children's individual goals.

- To encourage children's active participation.

- To emphasize the concept of the day.

Discussion of Demonstration

■ Did the children have to wait for the teacher to be ready?
(Scene 1, Scene 2)

■ Did the teacher give meaningful positive reinforcement?
(Scene 1, Scene 2)

■ Which scene provided the better learning experience?
(Scene 1, Scene 2)

Optimal Learning

In order for optimal learning to take place, the teacher has to be involved in the activity.

Reduce Waiting

When children get their own materials, waiting time is reduced.

Teaching Strategies

- Use positive reinforcement.

- Embed goals in activities.

- Be enthusiastic.

- Participate actively in activities.

- Prepare materials before activity.

- Teach through a blend of modeling and direct teaching.

Teacher's Role in Center Activities

- Encourage child choice.

- Encourage exploration and experimentation.

- Teach through modeling/direct teaching.

- Embed individual and general goals in the activities.

- Encourage child problem solving.

Teaching Strategies: Child Behaviors

- Make choices.

- Learn through doing.

- Be actively involved in stories.

- Enter into discussions.

- Problem solve.

- Flow from one center to another.

Preparing Ahead:
The Key to Success

■ Prepare to read the story.

■ Think about how you will involve the children in the story.

■ Learn the songs and raps in advance.

■ Plan to use the music/rap outside of Spark time.

■ Gather materials for story time and to introduce the centers.

Developing Children's Skills

■ Read through the activity.

■ Think about your children.

■ Ask yourself, "What can they learn by doing the activity?"

■ What skills can you promote?

■ How will you promote these skills?

■ How will you adapt for a child with special needs?

Thinking through an Activity

- What is the purpose of the activity?

- What can children learn by participating in it?

- How can you make it more enticing?

- What could you add or delete?

Importance of Reading Stories

Children begin to understand

- Importance of print

- Left to right progression

- Things they have never experienced

- How to share their experiences

- New words

- Art

Benefits of Involving Children at Story Time

- They are more attentive.

- They gain understanding of concepts.

- They become more aware of language structure used in the story.

- They gain understanding of new words.

Value of Story Repetition

Children

- Anticipate what is going to happen next.

- Generalize information.

- Learn to sequence events.

- Begin to understand conversational structure.

- May relate the story to their own experiences.

Value of Story Repetition (Continued)

Children

- Have an expanded attention span.

- Notice details in illustrations.

- Learn new concepts.

- Use more complex sentence structure.

Spark Story Time

- One story is repeated throughout the week.

- Children are encouraged to be verbally and physically involved in the story.

Promoting Children's Skill Development

- Ask open-ended questions.

- Ask questions that seek a specific answer.

- Discuss story.

- Have children demonstrate actions from the story.

Teachers' Comments

"The repetition brought out children's creativity, increased their language skills, and strengthened their recall and sequencing skills."

"The hand movements, verbal chants, etc., that are suggested for children to do during the story reading helped focus children's attention."

Three Basic Ways to Create an Environment of Acceptance

- Materials in the classroom

- Activities in the classroom

- Response to children's actions

Classroom Pictures Should Include:

- People of different color and race

- Both males and females in nonstereotypical roles and professions

- People with disabilities in active roles

- People of different ages in capable roles

Classroom Pictures Should Include (Continued)

- Different types of homes, such as houses, apartment buildings, and trailers

- Different types of home environments, such as urban and rural settings

- Various ethnic cultures

Sample Spark
Classroom Schedule

8:15 Arrival/Spark

8:45 Spark

9:45 Outdoor Play

10:15 Free Play

11:00 Large Group

11:15 Dismissal

Adaptations
(Teacher Suggestions)

- Implement music as a large-group activity.

- Use the units for two weeks (see resource list for additional books).

- Introduce project approach with a Spark unit.

  – *Anansi and the Moss-Covered Rock*: spiders

  – *The Very Quiet Cricket*: insects

What Stories Can I Put Together for a Theme?

Theme: Family

- *Baby Rattlesnake*

- *Jonathan and His Mommy*

- *No Fair to Tigers*

- *Mama, Do You Love Me?*

What Stories Can I Put Together for a Theme? (Continued)

Theme: Animals

- *The Bossy Gallito*

- *Polar Bear, Polar Bear, What Do You Hear?*

- *The Little Mouse, the Red Ripe Strawberry, and the Big Hungry Bear*

- *Nine-in-One Grr! Grr!*

To Promote Growth through Literacy and the Arts

Summary

- Prepare: avoid child waiting.

- Involve children in the story.

- Involve children in discussion.

- Make the introduction to centers enticing.

- Provide opportunities for child choice.

Summary (Continued)

- Be an active participant in activities.

- Embed individual goals in activities.

- Give meaningful positive reinforcement.

- Teach through a blend of modeling and direct teaching.

Teacher Comments

"I think the concept of teaching through the arts and music and make-believe is very appealing and very effective with the kids."

"I think the children really enjoy it and I certainly enjoy it. And overall I think they really learn a lot."

WORKSHOP 2

Using Spark Activities: Art

I. Instructions for the Spark Trainer

II. Training Script

Review of Spark Teaching Strategies (10 minutes)

Introduction to Spark Art Center Activities (15 minutes)

Activities That Are Meaningful to Children (30 minutes)

Exploring the Teaching Potential of Art Activities (45 minutes)

Learning to Teach and Adapt Spark Art Activities
   (approximately 120 minutes, depending
   on the number of participants)

Summary (10 minutes)

III. Handouts

IV. Overheads

I. Instructions for the Spark Trainer

Purpose

The purpose of the arts in-service training is to help teachers recognize the teaching opportunities inherent in arts activities for different developmental areas—gross motor, fine motor, cognitive, language, social/emotional—in general and in the Spark activities in particular. They will become aware of teaching strategies to use to promote optimal learning during arts activities, consider ways to embed children's goals in activities, and discuss how to adapt activities to meet individual needs.

Preparing for the Workshop

This workshop is intended for no more than thirty people. Since all participants take part in the implementation of small-group activities and model an activity for the rest of the group, the process becomes tedious if too many activities are enacted. Therefore, if it is necessary to train more than thirty people simultaneously, ask a cofacilitator to work with half the group during the implementation of the Spark activities (see Learning to Teach and Adapt Spark Art Activities, page 118). This way, the large group may be divided into two segments, each of which then breaks into small groups, which demonstrate their activities for their half of the large group.

The number of stories used in the team demonstration activity at the end of the workshop will depend upon the size of the training group. The activities are most successful if there are no more than seven participants in each small group. One activity has been selected from each of the stories. Trainers should read through the instructions at least twice before starting to prepare for the workshop.

☐ Gather materials listed for the workshop.

☐ Prepare overheads.

☐ Check the clarity of the first transparency on the overhead projector.

☐ Make copies of handouts.

☐ Set up the room for the first activity (Making a Product).

☐ Seat the participants in teaching teams.

☐ Place materials needed for activities where you can reach them easily.

Materials to Be Prepared and Gathered

☐ Overheads 127 and 201–218

☐ Timer (optional) to time activities

☐ Calculator (optional) to average goals

☐ Three pairs of scissors

☐ Tape

☐ Collage materials

☐ Base paper for collage

☐ Glue (four small squeeze containers)

☐ Construction paper of varying colors (enough for each participant to have one piece)

☐ Sand (at least four shaker containers of varying colors)

☐ Materials for the following Spark art center activities:

    ☐ *Anansi and the Moss-Covered Rock,* day 1

    ☐ *Big Al,* day 2

    ☐ *The Little Mouse, the Red Ripe Strawberry, and the Big Hungry Bear,* day 3

    ☐ *The Very Quiet Cricket,* day 4

☐ Blank transparencies and markers

Books

☐ *Anansi and the Moss-Covered Rock*

☐ *Baby Rattlesnake*

☐ *Big Al*

☐ *The Little Mouse, the Red Ripe Strawberry, and the Big Hungry Bear*

☐ *The Very Quiet Cricket*

Handouts

☐ Activity matrixes for the following Spark units (see Workshop 1 handouts), one per participant:

    ☐ *Anansi and the Moss-Covered Rock*

☐ *Big Al*

☐ *The Little Mouse, the Red Ripe Strawberry, and the Big Hungry Bear*

☐ *The Very Quiet Cricket*

☐ One copy each of the following Spark Activity pages:

   ☐ *Anansi and the Moss-Covered Rock,* Day 1, Art

   ☐ *Big Al,* Day 2, Art

   ☐ *The Little Mouse, the Red Ripe Strawberry, and the Big Hungry Bear,* Day 3, Art

   ☐ *The Very Quiet Cricket,* Day 4, Art

☐ Four copies of basket pattern (see handouts at the end of this workshop) copied on heavy paper or card stock

☐ Promoting Skills through Art

☐ Child Goals handouts, seven per participant (see appendix 2)

II. Training Script

Review of Spark Teaching Strategies

Show OH 201, Spark Art Workshop.
Show OH 127, Teaching Strategies.

As the participants are gathering, display overhead 201.

Review the teaching strategies for the Spark center activities. Also review the format of the curriculum. Remind the participants of the importance of reviewing the daily activities at the beginning of each story time and the value of story repetition.

Introduction to Spark Art Center Activities

Show OH 202, Goals of the Art Workshop.

State that the purpose of the workshop today is to learn about the Spark art center activities and how teachers can use them to work on children's individual and general skills.

Spark Art Centers

Show OH 203, Teaching Strategies for Art Activities; **show OH 127** again if needed.

Present the teaching strategies for art activities that are encouraged by the Spark curriculum. Ask the participants if they see any similarities between the strategies used during story time and the strategies used during the art activities. If necessary, display the strategies from Workshop 1 on overhead 127 again, pointing out the similarities. Say that the same teaching strategies are used in all parts of Spark. The intent is to promote child growth in all areas of development. This is done by using open-ended activities; by encouraging choices, exploration, and experimentation; and by embedding child goals in the activities.

With overhead 204 displayed, say that before the center activity starts

Show OH 204, Before the Center Activity Begins.

- the review of the previous day's activities has taken place,
- the story has been read,
- the concept of the day has been introduced,
- the centers have been introduced, and
- children have chosen the center they wish to go to first.

Activities That Are Meaningful to Children

Preschool Art Activities

Discuss the fact that typical early childhood classrooms use visual art activities because children are highly interested in them. Ask participants for a show of hands if they use art in their classrooms.

Discuss the types of art activities and materials they already use, such as painting, fingerpainting, playdough, and junk structures. Write the suggested activities on a blank overhead. Ask how often they use art activities. If the reply is every day, ask them to expand and give an example of what they do every day.

Use blank transparency to list art activities participants use.

Promoting Skill Development

With overhead 205 showing, say that you will talk about typical art activities and what developmental skills can be promoted through each one.

With overhead 206 showing, talk about the skills promoted through fingerpainting:

Show OH 205, Promoting Skills through Art.

Show OH 206, Finger-painting.

- fine motor (pincer grasp, eye-hand coordination, left-to-right progression, tactile awareness)
- cognitive (colors, shapes, meaningful counting, size relationships)
- language (labeling)
- social (sharing materials)

With overhead 207 showing, talk about each drawing tool and the developmental skills that can be promoted through each:

Show OH 207, Drawing with Markers, Pencils, Crayons.

- fine motor (pincer grasp, eye-hand coordination, left-to-right progression)

■ cognitive (colors, shapes, meaningful counting, size relationships, body parts)

■ language (labeling, conversational language)

■ social (sharing materials)

Show OH 208, Making Objects with Playdough.

With overhead 208 showing, talk about the developmental skills that can be promoted through activities with playdough:

■ fine motor (squeezing, rolling objects, pinching, eye-hand coordination, tactile awareness)

■ cognitive (size relationships, meaningful counting, labeling shapes, colors)

■ language (labeling, conversational language)

Show OH 209, Making Junk Structures.

With overhead 209 showing, talk about the developmental skills that can be promoted through making junk structures:

■ fine motor (manipulating objects, gluing or taping)

■ cognitive (problem solving, size relationships)

■ language (discussing work, labeling)

■ social (sharing materials, working with others)

Show OH 210, Painting.

With overhead 210 showing, talk about the developmental skills that can be promoted through painting:

■ fine motor (pincer grasp, eye-hand coordination, left-to-right progression)

■ cognitive (size relationships, meaningful counting, labeling shapes, colors)

■ social (sharing materials)

■ language (describing work)

Exploring the Teaching Potential of Art Activities

Demonstration: Making a Product

Introduce Child Goals handout.

State that there has just been a discussion of the many developmental goals that may be promoted during art activities. During the next demonstrations they will watch to see how many of the goals are addressed during the activity. Ask the participants to find the handouts titled Child Goals and remove one from their folders; show a sample if needed. Say that they have enough copies for all of the demonstrations that they will see.

Discuss the Child Goals handout, explaining that it lists developmental goals under each of the five domains. Say that as they watch the next activities, they should circle any goals on the handout that they see being addressed. Stress that they should only circle goals that are actually promoted, not ones that could be promoted, during the activity. At the end of each activity they will count the goals they circled and write the number in the upper-right corner of the paper.

Ask for three volunteers who will act like preschool children, and have them sit around a table at the front of the room where they have good working space. The other participants will be observers and should move if they need to in order to watch the demonstration and mark their goal sheets. Put all the needed materials in the middle of the table where all the volunteers can easily reach them. The volunteers will make a paper basket, cutting on designated lines, folding, and taping to make the completed product. (This activity is deliberately too complex for preschoolers; the purpose is to demonstrate that such activities do not meet the needs of preschool children and are a poor teaching tool.)

Tell the volunteers that they will each make a basket and that, although young children would have plenty of time to make the product, they will only have five minutes. Encourage them to get patterns and pairs of scissors. Before they start, give them the following explicit directions, one step at a time, and show them a prepared model:

- Cut across the end of the paper on the bold line to make the handle.

- Cut on the dotted lines, just to the end of the dotted line.

- Fold on the bold lines.

- Tape the sides of the basket together.

- Tape the handle to the inside of the basket.

- Display the model on the table where everyone can see it.

Thank the volunteers, and instruct the observers to tally their goals on their Child Goals handouts. Ask one person to add the goals from all the handouts (a calculator is very helpful) and divide by the number of participants. You will record the number on overhead 211. While the calculations are taking place, use overhead 212 to guide a discussion of what children learn from the basket activity. Ask if the activity was developmentally appropriate. Why not? What was wrong with it? What developmental skills were promoted during this activity as children made the product? Discuss why these types of activities are used in preschool classrooms. The reason is often that parents expect them.

Conduct paper-basket activity.

Give directions. Show model. Allow five minutes.

Record goals tally on OH 211, Average Goals. Show OH 212, Demonstration: Making a Product, and discuss.

Start collage activity; leave volunteers alone for five minutes.

Write average goals number on OH 211.

Show OH 213, Demonstration: Open-Ended Activity, No Teacher Participation; discuss.

Read *Baby Rattlesnake.* **Remind observers to mark their goal sheets. Ask for volunteers. Conduct Spark Activity with volunteers. Teach through the activity.**

Demonstration: Open-Ended Activity, No Teacher Participation

Clear away the basket materials and set out materials to make a collage. Ask for three new volunteers to act like preschool children. Remind the observers to mark new goal sheets as they observe the next demonstration. Remind them to circle only the goals that they see being addressed. Ask the volunteers to sit around the table. Instruct them to use the materials in any way they wish to make a collage; when you have given the instructions, walk away. After five minutes, thank the volunteers and gather the materials.

Thank the volunteers; ask the observers to tally their goals and the helper to tally the group total. Write the average score on the Average Goals overhead.

Use overhead 213 to guide a discussion about the collage demonstration: If children were participating in this activity, what developmental skills would have been promoted? How could the activity be adapted to meet individual needs of children? What else could you do with this activity?

Demonstration: Spark Art Activity

For this demonstration, you will use the art activity from day 2 of the *Baby Rattlesnake* unit. Before you start this activity, arrange four chairs around the table and place the supplies for the activity in the middle of the table. Read *Baby Rattlesnake* to the group and then ask for three volunteers to act as preschool children. Sit at the table with them and participate in the activity. Encourage the volunteers to join in discussing the story by asking such questions as, "Where did Baby Rattlesnake live? Have you ever been to the desert?" Help them to understand that deserts are very dry. Ask them to show with their hands how snakes move. Ask what kind of a trail they think a snake would make where it is very dry. Tell them that they are going to make trails on their papers like Baby Rattlesnake might have made as he traveled through the desert.

Encourage them to get their own materials, choosing the color of paper they want to use, a container of glue, and a shaker of colored sand. Join in the activity, modeling making curved lines with the glue and shaking sand on them. As you shake the sand, say, "Shake, shake, shake. I'm shaking my sand the way Baby Rattlesnake shook his tail." As you work, discuss the colors of paper and sand that the "children" are using, how the glue feels, how it feels with the sand shaken on it, and whether their trails are curved or straight, long or short. Encourage them to make any type of trail they wish to, and to count the number of trails they make. Encourage sharing or trading of materials, and model saying "please" and "thank you." Ask what kind of animal made their trails, and where the trails are going. Compare which trails are similar and which are different. Give positive reinforcement as you work.

Tally goals, and write the average on OH 211. Compare the numbers of child goals promoted during the activities.

Use overhead 214 to guide a discussion: What general developmental skills were promoted through the activity? How could the activity be adapted to meet children's individual needs? What else could be done with the activity? What could teachers do to make the activity more challenging? Include such suggestions as:

- Glue with different widths of paintbrushes

- Compare glitter, confetti, colored sand

- Use light and dark paper; compare trails

- Make two trails the same, then one different

Stress that although the Spark art activities often have some type of product, each child's product will be different. It isn't important what the final product looks like; the activity is simply an opportunity to promote children's skills while they are engaged in an activity they enjoy. Teachers are encouraged to change materials in the classroom to fit the needs of their children.

Compare Activities for Their Contributions to Child Growth

Use overhead 215 to compare the different components of the activities just completed. Say that you have explored the teaching possibilities of three different types of art activities. Stress that visual art activities for children are often either a teacher-designed product or a free-choice activity without teacher participation.

With overhead 216 displayed, say that product activities may not meet the diverse needs of all the children in the group. They may either stress skills that some children have already acquired or require skills that some children do not have.

With overhead 217 displayed, say that free-choice art activities provide children with opportunities to pursue areas of interest. However, since teachers are usually not involved in the activity, golden opportunities for teaching may be missed.

Enter goals total on OH 211.

Show OH 214 Demonstration: Spark Activity, and discuss.

Show OH 211 and discuss.

Show OH 215, Typical Preschool Art.

Show OH 216, Product Activities.

Show OH 217, Free-Choice Art Activities.

State that, like all other activities, art activities for children should be developmentally appropriate so children can participate fully in the activity and receive the most benefit from the activity.

Most open-ended art activities, such as painting, drawing, working with playdough, and building structures, are developmentally appropriate for young children.

Learning to Teach and Adapt Spark Art Activities

Introduce the Activity

Review stories and themes.

Review the stories in *Anansi and the Moss-Covered Rock; Big Al; The Little Mouse, the Red Ripe Strawberry, and the Big Hungry Bear;* and *The Very Quiet Cricket.* Ask the participants to look at the activity matrix for each story. Discuss the daily themes that have been drawn from each of the stories: *Anansi* (cover, behind/in front of, spiders, all), *Big Al* (ocean, making friends, same/different, strong) *The Little Mouse, the Red Ripe Strawberry, and the Big Hungry Bear* (hear, see, smell, colors, half, share); and *The Very Quiet Cricket* (rubbing, big/little, together, insects).

Tell the participants that they will be divided into teams. Each team will select a leader to be the teacher. The rest of the group will pretend to be preschool children. They should prepare to present an assigned Spark activity as it is written. They should assume that the story has been read and the concept introduced already. They will have twenty minutes to prepare their activity and ten minutes to present it. Each team will present its activity for the large group. During each presentation, the people who are not presenting will mark their goals sheets as they observe.

Facilitate the Activity

Watch presentations. Collect and tabulate goals sheets.

Divide the group into teams; create four teams if possible. Assign each team one of the four art activities you have prepared. Encourage participants to prepare to teach a section of the activity, selecting materials they need to set up their activity from the materials you have gathered for their use. As the teams begin to prepare for the activity, go to each team, giving help as needed and encouraging them to think what developmental goals they could promote during the activity and to do a brief run-through of the activity before presenting it to the large group. (Assign activities to teams; distribute materials; allow preparation time.)

Have each teaching team lead its activity as the other participants observe and mark their goal sheets. After each presentation, lead the group in applause, then collect and tabulate the goal sheets.

Discuss the Presentations

With overhead 218 displayed, tell participants to use the questions on the overhead for self-evaluation. Work through the questions together: Did I ask questions during the activity? Did I try to promote child learning during the activity? Did I remember to consider possible cultural differences? What could I have done better?

Compliment the teaching teams for doing an excellent job. Say that no two activities would have the same number of child goals embedded in the activity, but all of the teams promoted many goals. Read the average scores of each team's activity to reinforce the impact that Spark activities have on child growth.

Summary

State that much more can be done with art activities than is typically done in many preschool classrooms. Tell participants that they have a handout titled Promoting Skills through Art Activities that provides information about how to help children develop their cognitive, fine-motor, language, social, and preliteracy skills through art. State that one of the most important benefits of open-ended art activities is that the activities can accommodate many developmental levels since there is no wrong or right way to do the activity.

Review Spark teaching strategies for art activities. State that the primary purpose of the Spark art activities is to use activities that are highly interesting to young children in order to promote children's development.

Show OH 218, Thinking through the Activity.

Compliment teams.
Report scores.

Refer to the handout Promoting Skills through Art.

Review Spark teaching strategies; show **OH 127** if needed.

Anansi and the Moss-Covered Rock
Day 1: Art Center

What to Do:

Relate the activity to the story. Remind the children that Anansi the Spider found a magic moss-covered rock. Say that they are going to make their own covered rocks, but that their rocks might be glitter-covered rocks, or cloth-covered rocks. They may cover their rocks with different things.

Cover the rocks with paint. Demonstrate painting a rock, as you encourage the children to cover their own rocks with paint. As everyone paints, prompt discussion about how shiny the paint looks, the color of the paint mixture, and how the children are making the rocks look like moss-covered rocks. When they are finished, put them aside to dry.

Cover boxes and rocks with different materials. Put out the boxes and unpainted rocks, the glue, and the materials for covering the boxes. Invite the children to cover their boxes and rocks with any of the materials they wish to use. Join in and model covering a rock or a box completely. Ask the children to describe their decorated rocks or boxes ("a cotton-covered box," or "a rock covered with paper and glitter").

Change the covered table into a clean one. When the children are finished, remark that the table is covered with many things. Have the children name all the things on the table. Then ask them to change the covered table into a clean one.

MATERIALS

- Rocks, two or more for each child and each adult
- Paintbrushes
- Paint mixture (combine 2 tablespoons liquid starch, 2 tablespoons water, 1 tablespoon green paint powder or food coloring, and ½ cup salt)
- Small boxes, one or more for each child and each adult
- Glue
- Materials for covering rocks and boxes, such as cotton balls, sand, glitter, Styrofoam chips, tissue paper, shiny paper, wrapping paper, newspaper, scraps of cloth

Big Al

Day 2: Art Center

What to Do:

Relate the activity to the story. Remind the children that Big Al wanted to be friends with the other fish. He tried very hard to make friends. Say that one thing some people do with their friends is to go boating together. Say that they are going to make a boat and that they will all work together as they paint and decorate the boat. Suggest that another way to make friends is to do things together and share materials.

Paint a large box together. Provide a variety of paint, brushes, pieces of decorative papers, glue, and markers. Work with the children to paint and decorate the boat. Encourage the children to discuss experiences they may have had with boats as they work. Ask them if they have ever been in a boat. What kind of boat was it? Who were they with? Did they go fishing?

Encourage working together and sharing. As you work with the children emphasize that everyone is working together and sharing materials with their friends. Encourage children to ask one another for materials and praise children who share.

Name the boat. Tell the children that boats often have names. Ask them to suggest a name for their boat. Paint the name on the boat.

Save the boat. Save the boat for day 3 make-believe and day 5 large-group activities.

MATERIALS

- Rectangular box, preferably large enough for two children to sit in
- Paint
- Paintbrushes
- Markers
- Decorative strips of paper
- Glue

The Little Mouse, the Red Ripe Strawberry, and the Big Hungry Bear
Day 3: Art Center

What to Do:

Relate the activity to the story. Remind the children that the mouse cut the strawberry in half and shared it with his friend. Say that their food has already been cut in half and they are going to paint with half a piece of food.

Match and name food halves. Show the pieces of food to the children. Encourage them to fit the matching pieces together. Say that when something is cut in half, both pieces are the same size. They are the same, not different. Encourage the children to name each item.

Let the children experiment freely with the materials. Place the paint, paper, and food pieces where they are easily accessible, and join in the activity. Encourage the children to compare the prints made by different pieces of food. Which food makes the biggest print? If you use both halves, does the print look the same or different? If you print over a print you already made with a different color, what happens? Does the print change color or stay the same?

MATERIALS

- Pieces of fruit or vegetables, cut in half
- Thick paint, red, yellow, and blue
- Paper (several different colors to provide choice)

The Very Quiet Cricket
Day 4: Art Center

What to Do:

Relate the activity to the story. Remind the children that the little cricket was an insect and that all insects have six legs. Show them the pictures of insects and help them trace the antennae on the insects and count their body parts. Point out the eyes and mouths on the insects. Say that they will make their own insects any way they want to make them.

Show how to make insects. Place the materials out where they are easily accessible. Join the children as they get boxes or Styrofoam balls to make the bodies of their insects. Place pictures of insects around where they can be easily seen. Show how to put the body pieces together (toothpicks in Styrofoam balls, or glue between boxes) and how to stick various materials onto the insect. Glitter can be used for fireflies; pieces of shiny metallic paper make nice-looking beetles. Encourage creativity.

Make more insects. Encourage the children to work together in pairs to make additional insects. Encourage variety, stressing that there are many different kinds of insects in the world.

Make a display. Make a display of the insects and encourage each child to say where her insect lives and how it moves.

MATERIALS

- Styrofoam balls
- Small boxes
- Pipe stems
- Craft sticks
- Collage materials such as glitter, pieces of felt, spangles, ribbons
- Glue
- Toothpicks

Promoting Skills through Art

Cognitive Development

Art activities provide an opportunity for children to learn a variety of cognitive skills in a hands-on format. When children participate in art activities they encounter color, shape, texture, size, and form. They learn about cause and effect—for example, when they mix two colors of paint, the color changes. They learn about size through observing thick and thin lines, large and small balls of clay, heavy or light materials for sculptures. They learn about physical laws—for example, sculptures that are not balanced fall over, and paint drips down the paper on an easel. They learn about patterns by painting a pattern of dots and lines, or by making a row of balls and snakes with playdough. They also develop their problem-solving skills when they make decisions about how to attach one material to another or how to balance their sculptures.

Promoting Cognitive Skills through Art Activities

- Allow children to experiment with art materials and encourage them to talk about what they are doing. Talking about the experience helps the children understand what has happened and gives meaning to the experience.

- Allow children to solve problems on their own, but offer help when a child seems discouraged. For example, if some children use so much water when they paint that it creates holes in the paper, encourage them to figure out

how they made the holes. However, if a child wants to stop painting because the paper is "icky" with holes in it, help the child realize that water made the holes, and show him how to paint without using so much water.

- Encourage the children to predict what will happen. Before a child mixes red and yellow playdough, ask what will happen to it; or before a child opens a folded blot paper, ask her what she thinks it will look like.

- Let children repeat activities. Children learn concepts by experiencing them over and over. By seeing the same results whenever they do a particular activity, children learn that physical laws are constant. Children with cognitive limitations in particular need to encounter concepts many times before they master them. However, if a child seems to need a boost to go on to the next level of learning, pair him with a child at a slightly higher level to serve as a model.

Fine-Motor Development

Children develop physically from the head downward and from the shoulders out. At first they use the whole arm for fine-motor control. Through maturation and practice, they eventually are able to rotate the wrist and then use their fingers for controlling fine-motor tools, such as pencils, paintbrushes, and crayons.

Twos and young threes use whole-arm movements. They need space to work in, space for whole-arm movement. They need large pieces of paper, large brushes with wide handles, large crayons, or large pencils. Drawing on paper helps them learn to control their movements in order to confine a drawing to a small space. After threes begin to rotate the wrist to control their art tools, they can begin to use smaller paper and narrower tools.

Typical fours and fives begin to use finger control. They can use fine-point pens and pencils and smaller paper (note cards are fun for this age group).

Promoting Fine-Motor Skills through Art Activities

▪ Provide materials that are developmentally appropriate. If there are children with several levels of development in one group, provide a variety of utensils and paper sizes and encourage each child to use materials with which he will experience the most success.

▪ Give encouraging, specific feedback. Hearing you talk about lines, shapes, and drawings that she has created helps the child recognize her abilities and encourages her to continue to form those figures.

▪ Give suggestions when a child seems frustrated. When a child says, "I can't do it!" she is usually attempting something that is too difficult. Suggest something more appropriate for her to try and help her appreciate the value of those things she is able to do. For example, if she is having difficulty cutting you might provide physical assistance, start the cutting for her, or show her how to practice by fringing the edge of the paper.

Social Development

Children learn to interact with other as they work together, observe what the other children are doing, talk about what they are doing, share materials and space, and work together to create a project.

Twos and young threes tend to work side by side, using the same materials and observing each other from time to time or exchanging materials. This type of interaction relates to their level of play development.

Older threes, fours, and fives talk to each other about what they are doing, exchanging ideas and sharing materials. They often enjoy working on such art projects as building a box sculpture together.

Promoting Social Skills through Art Activities

▪ Provide space for children to work near each other and where they can see each other's work. Encourage them to work on tables rather than on easels.

▪ Supply plenty of basic materials so that children do not have a reason to argue over them. If you include special materials such as staplers that children need to share, be sure that children also have other things such as scissors and paper to use while they are waiting their turn.

▪ If arguments arise, let children try to resolve the conflicts on their own. Step in only if things get out of hand. Help children resolve conflicts by asking them to tell each other what happened, how they felt about it, and what they want from the other person, instead of by imposing a solution.

- Comment on individual children's artwork while everyone is working. "You made your playdough look bumpy. How did you do that?" This will encourage children to look to each other for ideas, and help them learn to appreciate the creativity of others. However, avoid comparing the work of children.

- Plan projects which encourage children to work together. Even twos and young threes can participate if they have a part of the project to work on alone. For example, if children are painting a mural together, you might draw a large square on the paper for a young child to paint.

Preliteracy Development

Art is the earliest form of symbolic expression that people use. At first children scribble and experiment with art tools with no plans for forming pictures and messages. As they mature and practice, they gradually begin to realize that people can use pictures to represent objects and to express ideas. This understanding that people can use symbols is a necessary step towards the ability to read and write. Also, art activities help children develop the visual discrimination skills needed for identifying letters and numbers.

Children practice language skills when they talk about what they are doing, ask each other questions, and listen to directions on how to use materials. They might also dictate stories about artwork that they have completed.

As twos and young threes experiment with art materials, they develop fine-motor skills needed for mature visual discrimina-

tion. They usually use art materials spontaneously with no preplanned intentions. However, they begin to realize that pictures can represent real things. They are able to form circles, lines, and some other shapes as they work, but often they cannot make these shapes upon request. This ability takes practice.

Older threes, fours, and fives realize that they can create symbols of things, events, and ideas. They enjoy talking about their artwork for an adult to record and like to sign their names to identify themselves as creators. They enjoy making a variety of basic shapes over and over, a natural way to practice visual discrimination skills.

Promoting Preliteracy through Art Activities

- Model using language as you talk with the child about what he is doing: "You are painting all over the paper."

- Ask questions that encourage a child to use language at her ability level. For example, if a three-year-old is rolling a piece of clay, you might ask, "Is your clay long or short? How did you do that?" If the child is five, you might ask, "How did you make such a long piece of clay?"

- Label the shapes that children make spontaneously to help them recognize their ability to make small defined forms and, eventually, letters.

- Ask children to tell you about their artwork. When a two- or three-year-old says, "It's a monster," he probably had no intention of making a monster as he worked. But by labeling artwork he begins to be aware of his own ability to create symbols. After children have had practice labeling drawings they have already made, they begin to plan ahead for the symbols they will create.

- Ask fours and fives to tell what they plan to do with art materials as they begin to work, or to tell what else they could do when they have been working for a while. Because language and thinking are so closely linked, this will help children develop cognitive skills (problem solving, logic, and reasoning) as well as language.

- Invite fours and fives to dictate stories about their work for you to write down and then read back to them. This is an extremely valuable prereading experience. Children learn that letters are used for forming words, and that they can record their own ideas using written language.

- Display the children's artwork at their eye level and encourage them to talk about it.

- Record what children say about their artwork and read it back to them. This helps children understand that people use letters to represent words.

Spark Art Workshop

Teaching through the Visual Arts

Goals of the Art Workshop

- To identify skills taught through the arts.

- To learn to teach Spark center activities.

- To identify adaptations for individual children.

Teaching Strategies for Arts Activities

- Use positive reinforcement.

- Embed general and individual goals in activities.

- Be an enthusiastic, active participant.

- Teach through a blend of modeling and direct teaching.

- Encourage choices, exploration, experimentation, and problem solving.

Before the Center Activity Begins

- Review of previous day has been done

- Story has been read

- Concept of the day has been introduced

- The centers have been introduced

- Children have chosen a center

Promoting Skills through Art

Fingerpainting

- Fine Motor (coordination, tactile awareness)

- Cognitive (colors, shapes, meaningful counting, size relationships)

- Language (labeling, describing objects, conversation)

- Social (sharing materials, discussing others' work)

Drawing with Markers, Pencils, Crayons

- Fine motor (pincer grasp, eye-hand coordination, left-to-right progression)

- Cognitive (colors, shapes, meaningful counting, size relationships, body parts)

- Language (labeling)

- Social (sharing materials)

Making Objects with Playdough

- Fine Motor (squeezing, rolling objects, pinching, eye-hand coordination, tactile awareness)

- Cognitive (size relationships, meaningful counting, labeling, shapes, colors)

- Language (labeling, conversational language)

Making Junk Structures

- Fine Motor (manipulating objects, gluing, taping)

- Cognitive (problem solving, size relationships)

- Language (describing work, labeling)

- Social (sharing materials, working with others)

Painting

- Fine Motor (pincer grasp, eye-hand coordination, left-to-right progression)

- Cognitive (size relationships, meaningful counting, labeling shapes, colors)

- Social (sharing materials)

- Language (describing work)

Average Goals

- Product _____

- Free Play _____

- Spark _____

Demonstration: Making a Product

- Was the activity developmentally appropriate?

- What developmental skills were promoted when the children made the product?

Demonstration: Open-Ended Activity, No Teacher Participation

■ What developmental skills of children were promoted during this activity?

■ How could the activity be adapted to meet the needs of individual children?

■ What else could you do with this activity?

Demonstration: Spark Art Activity

- What developmental skills of children were promoted during the Spark activity?

- How could you have adapted this activity for individual children in your classroom?

- What else could you do with this activity?

Typical Preschool Art

Typical preschool art is often either

- a teacher-designed product or

- a free-choice activity without teacher participation

Product Activities

May not meet the diverse needs of all the children in the group:

- Too simple for some children

- Too difficult for some children

Free-Choice Art Activities

Golden opportunities for teaching may be missed.

Thinking through the Activity

- Did I ask questions during the activity?

- Did I try to promote child learning?

- Did I consider possible cultural differences?

- What could I have done better?

WORKSHOP 3

Using Spark Activities: Make-Believe

I. Instructions for the Spark Trainer

II. Training Script

III. Handouts

IV. Overheads

I. Instructions for the Spark Trainer

Purpose

The purpose of the make-believe center workshop is to help teachers learn how to implement the Spark creative arts make-believe center activities and to use these activities as a way to work on children's individual and general skills. They will become aware of teaching strategies to use to promote optimal learning during make-believe activities, consider ways to embed children's goals in activities, and discuss how to adapt activities to meet individual needs.

Preparing for the Workshop

This workshop is intended for no more than thirty people. Since all participants take part in the implementation of small-group activities and model an activity for the rest of the group, the process becomes tedious if too many activities are enacted. Therefore, if it is necessary to train more than thirty people simultaneously, ask a cofacilitator to work with half the group during the implementation of the Spark activities. This way, the large group may be divided into two segments, each of which then breaks into small groups and demonstrates their activities for their half of the large group.

The number of stories used in the final team demonstration will depend upon the size of the training group. The activities are most successful if there are no more than seven participants in each small group. One activity has been selected from each of the stories.

The following preparations will help make the workshop a success. Trainers should read through the instructions at least twice before starting to prepare for the workshop.

☐ Gather materials listed for the workshop.

☐ Prepare overheads.

☐ Set up overhead projector.

☐ Check the clarity of the first overhead on the overhead projector.

☐ Make copies of handouts.

☐ Set up the room for the first activity.

☐ Place materials needed for activities where you can reach them easily.

☐ Seat participants in teaching teams.

☐ Leave room at the front of the room for demonstrations.

Materials to Be Prepared and Gathered

☐ Overhead 203 (from Workshop 2) and overheads 301 to 317

☐ For free play and facilitated free play demonstrations:

    ☐ Large trash bag of shredded paper

    ☐ Old sheet

☐ For Spark make-believe activity:

    ☐ Paper for children to tear

    ☐ Dress-up clothes, including coats, scarves, mittens, hats

    ☐ Large, heavy piece of cardboard with rope attached (sled); shovel

    ☐ Dolls

☐ Sample Child Goals handout

☐ Timer (optional)

☐ Calculator (optional)

Spark Books

☐ *Baby Rattlesnake*

☐ *If You Give a Pig a Pancake*

☐ *Jamela's Dress*

☐ *The Napping House*

☐ Materials for the following Spark make-believe center activities:

    ☐ *Baby Rattlesnake*, day 3

    ☐ *If You Give Pig a Pancake*, day 3

    ☐ *Jamela's Dress*, day 2

    ☐ *The Napping House*, day 1

☐ Blank transparencies and markers

Handouts

☐ One copy each of the following Spark Activity sheets:

☐ *Baby Rattlesnake,* Day 3, Make-Believe

☐ *If You Give a Pig a Pancake,* Day 3, Make-Believe

☐ *Jamela's Dress,* Day 2, Make-Believe

☐ *The Napping House,* Day 1, Make-Believe

☐ *The Snowy Day,* Day 2, Make-Believe

☐ Developmentally Appropriate Activities in Make-Believe

☐ Child Goals, six per participant (see appendix 2)

II. Training Script

Introduction to Spark Make-Believe Center Activities

Show OH 301, Spark Make-Believe Workshop.

With overhead 301 showing, state that the purpose of the workshop is to learn how teachers can use the Spark make-believe center activities to promote children's individual and general skills. Say that the center activities have children's general developmental skills embedded in them. When implemented as written, these activities will promote many of the children's general skills. They should also be used to promote children's individual skill development. Remind them that before the make-believe activity starts,

▨ the review of the previous day's activities has taken place,

▨ the story has been read,

▨ the concept of the day has been introduced,

▨ the centers have been introduced, and

▨ children have chosen the center they want to go to first.

Make-Believe Versus Dramatic Play

Discuss the terms "dramatic play" versus "make-believe," stating that make-believe is the Spark version (which is often a simpler version) of dramatic play.

Teaching Strategies for Make-Believe Activities

Show OH 302, Teaching Strategies for Make-Believe; compare with **OH 203,** Teaching Strategies for Art Activities (see workshop 2).

Use overhead 302 to discuss the Spark teaching strategies for make-believe activities. Ask the participants if they see any similarities between the strategies used during art activities and the strategies used during the make-believe activities; point out that the strategies are the same. If necessary, display overhead 203 from the previous workshop, stressing that the teaching strategies remain the same throughout the Spark center activities.

Activities That Are Meaningful to Children

Children's Interest in Make-Believe Activities

Discuss the fact that typical early childhood classrooms use make-believe activities because children are highly interested in this type of activity. Ask the participants if they use make-believe in their classrooms. If you are training several people, model raising your hand to ask for a show of hands.

Discuss the types of make-believe activities they use, such as housekeeping, role play, block corners, vehicle play, water play, sand-table play, doll play, and acting out stories. Write the suggested activities on a blank transparency. Ask how often they encourage the children to engage in make-believe activities. If the reply is every day, ask them to expand and give an example of what they do every day. Ask if their make-believe play is primarily free play. If so, how are they, as teachers, involved in the play?

Discuss overhead 303, giving examples of skills that may be promoted through housekeeping play.

Discuss overhead 304, giving examples of skills that may be promoted through role-playing.

Discuss overhead 305, giving examples of skills that may be promoted through play in the block corner.

Discuss overhead 306, giving examples of skills that may be promoted through vehicle play.

Discuss overhead 307, giving examples of skills that may be promoted through water-table play.

State that, like all other activities, make-believe activities for children should be developmentally appropriate in order for children to participate fully in the activity and to get the optimum benefit from it.

An activity used in many preschool programs is to have the children act out a favorite classroom story; however, typical three- and four-year-old children shouldn't be expected to act out an entire story. They may be able to pretend to be a single animal or other character in a story.

Ask if participants use make-believe activities.

On blank transparency, list make-believe activities already used; discuss.

Show OH 303, Housekeeping.

Show OH 304, Role-Play.

Show OH 305, Block Corner.

Show OH 306, Vehicle Play.

Show OH 307, Water-Table Play.

Exploring the Learning Potential of Make-Believe Activities

State that the participants have now identified many developmental goals that can be promoted during make-believe activities. During the next demonstrations, they will watch to see how many child goals are addressed during each activity. Show a sample Child Goals handout and direct participants to find their copies in their folders and have them ready. Say that they have enough copies of the handout for each of the activities that they will see.

Introduce Child Goals handout.

Discuss the Child Goals handout, explaining that it contains developmental goals listed under each of the five domains. Say that as they watch the demonstrations, they should circle any goals on the handout that they see being addressed. Stress that they should circle only goals that are actually promoted, not ones that could be promoted, during the activity. At the end of each activity they will count the goals they circled and write the number in the upper-right corner of their paper.

Demonstration: Free Play

Conduct free-play activity with sheet and "snow."

Scatter the shredded paper on the old sheet and ask for three volunteers to pretend to be preschool children. The other participants will be observers and should move so that they can see the activity and mark their goal sheets as they observe. Tell the participants that much make-believe in typical preschool classrooms happens during free play. Acknowledge that children can learn many things during free play, and that this demonstration will show a free-play make-believe activity. Ask the volunteers to pretend to be playing in the snow. Do not participate in the activity.

Thank volunteers and tally goals. Show OH 308, Free-Play Activity, and discuss.

After approximately five minutes, thank the volunteers. Ask the observers to tally their goals on their Child Goals handouts. To avoid making participants wait, ask one person to add the goals for the whole group (a calculator is very helpful) and divide by the number of participants. Record the resulting number on a blank transparency. While the calculations are being done, discuss the demonstration using overhead 308. Help the participants see that more goals would have been promoted if an adult had been present in the activity.

Demonstration: Facilitated Free Play

Ask for volunteers, conduct facilitated free play.

Ask for three new volunteers to play the roles of preschool children. Remind the observers to mark fresh goal sheets as they observe the activity. Remind them to circle only goals that they see being addressed. Ask the volunteers to again pretend to be preschool children playing with snow. Join the activity. Follow the children's lead, and help develop the play.

After approximately five minutes, thank the volunteers. Again, ask the observers to tally their goals and the helper to total them. Write the average score on the blank overhead. Use overhead 309 to lead a discussion of the activity.

Tally and record goals.
Show OH 309, Facilitated Free-Play Activity, and discuss.

Demonstration: Spark Make-Believe Activity

Tell the participants that you will now lead a Spark make-believe activity. Ask them to look at the *Snowy Day* day 2 activity sheet in their folders. Again, ask for volunteers and remind observers to mark the Child Goals handouts. Lead the *Snowy Day*, day 2 make-believe activity.

Lead *The Snowy Day*, day 2 make-believe activity.

Demonstrate teaching strategies throughout the planned activity: ask both closed and open-ended questions, give positive reinforcement, and promote skill development. Promote both the skills that are embedded in the activity and additional skills that might fit the child's individual needs as indicated by the behavior of the volunteer.

After the demonstration, thank the volunteers and ask the observers to tally their goals. While the helper averages the goals, use overhead 310 to lead a discussion of the activity. Record the averaged goals on the blank transparency with the scores from the first two demonstrations. Compare the results. Discuss the differences in the learning potential of the activities. Stress again that each of the three types of activities has its place in the preschool classroom.

Show OH 310, Spark Make-Believe Activity. Compare goals in demonstrations.

Summarize Make-Believe in Spark

Say that all Spark activities are linked to the story of the week and the theme of the day and thus are an integral part of the curriculum. Say that Spark make-believe activities include any scenario where children are engaged in open-ended pretend play. These include such activities as sand table, water table, block corner, vehicles, puppets, housekeeping, and acting out scenes from the story.

Show OH 311, Spark Make-Believe.

Remind the participants that day 5 activities are not in the usual Spark format but instead are more involved make-believe activities. The day 5 activities are loosely connected to the unit and go into more detail. For example, the children may be encouraged to work together to create and play in a post office, a pizza parlor, a restaurant, or a circus.

Talk about day 5 activities.

Learning to Teach and Adapt Spark Make-Believe Activities

Review the stories and themes of *Baby Rattlesnake* (family, shake, close, snakes), *If You Give a Pig a Pancake* (pancakes, sticky, homesick, under), *Jamela's Dress* (patterns, special, fold, feelings), and *The Napping House* (on/off, falling down, counting, happy).

Team Demonstration

Review stories, discuss themes; create teams; distribute activities and materials.

Tell the participants that they will be divided into teams of no more than seven. Each team will select a leader to be the teacher. The rest of the group will pretend to be preschool children. They should prepare to present an assigned Spark activity as it is written. They will have twenty minutes to prepare their activity and ten minutes to present it to the larger group. The people who are not presenting will mark the Child Goal handouts as they observe the activity. Divide the group into teaching teams. Assign one of the make-believe activity worksheets to each team and distribute the materials for the activity.

Help teams prepare.

Encourage participants to read through and prepare to teach the activity. As the teams begin to prepare for the activity, go to each team, give help as needed, and encourage participants to think about what developmental goals they could promote during the activity. Suggest that they briefly practice the activity before presenting it to the larger group.

Have teams present, observers mark goals. Tabulate goals.

Have each teaching team present its activity as the other participants observe and mark their Child Goals handouts. If possible, set a timer for ten minutes for each activity. This strategy establishes a clear time limit that everyone will accept. After each demonstration, lead the group in applause and collect and tabulate the goal sheets.

Show OH 312, Thinking through the Activity; discuss.

Work through the questions on overhead 312 together: Did I ask questions during the activity? Did I try to promote child learning during the activity? Did I consider possible cultural differences? What could I have done better?

Compliment teams. Report scores.

Compliment the teaching teams for doing an excellent job. Say that no two activities would have the same number of child goals embedded in the activity, but all of the teams promoted many goals. Read the average scores of each team's activity to reinforce the impact that Spark activities have on child growth.

Summary

Summarize by repeating that children's interest in make-believe provides an opportunity for teachers to promote many child skills during make-believe activities. Repeat that open-ended make-believe activities provide an excellent opportunity to meet the needs of children with diverse skills. Stress that preschool personnel know that there are many incentives to encourage preschool children to engage in make-believe activities. However, adults can enrich the make-believe setting in many ways. Use overheads 313, 314a and b, and 315 to summarize Spark make-believe.

Use overhead 316 to discuss appropriate types of make-believe activities for young children. Refer to the handout Developmentally Appropriate Activities in Make-Believe as a resource.

With overhead 317 displayed, stress again that the purpose of the Spark make-believe activities, like the Spark art activities, is to provide activities that are interesting to children to promote development of general as well as individual skills.

Show OH 313, Promoting Language through Dramatic Play, **314a** and **b,** Adult Involvement in Dramatic Play, and **315,** Promote Abstract Thinking. Discuss.

Show OH 316, Developmentally Appropriate Make-Believe, and discuss.

Show OH 317, Summary.

Baby Rattlesnake
Day 3: Make-Believe Center

What to Do:

Relate the activity to the story. Ask the children what Baby Rattlesnake hid in when he wanted to play his jokes. If necessary, show them the picture in the book that shows Baby Rattlesnake hiding in the rocks waiting for the chief's daughter. Say that they will make pretend rock piles.

Make pretend rock piles. Work with the children to use the empty boxes or classroom building materials to make big and little structures. Pretend that the structures are "rock" piles for Baby Rattlesnake to hide behind.

Act out part of the story. Encourage the children to take turns being Baby Rattlesnake as various animals and the chief's daughter come closer and closer to the rock.

Encourage the children to imitate other animals. Show the children the page in the book where Baby Rattlesnake is playing his joke on different animals. Encourage them to label an animal and then move like the animal as they come closer and closer to the rocks. Ask them what animal they are pretending to be. What sound does that animal make? Can they make the sound while they move as the animal moves? Ask them what other kind of animal they could be. Write down their suggestions, then encourage them to move as the different animals would move.

If You Give a Pig a Pancake
Day 3: Make-Believe Center

What to Do:

MATERIALS
- Book, *If You Give a Pig a Pancake*
- Several suitcases
- Bandannas and sticks
- Dress-up clothes

Relate the activity to the story. Ask the children why the pig was homesick. Ask if they have ever felt homesick. Encourage the children to share their experiences. Say that sometimes when people feel homesick it makes them feel better to go home for a little while. Say that they are going to pretend to pack to go home.

Show the materials. Show the children the materials and say that they can use either the regular suitcases or the kind of suitcase the pig used in the story. Show them the picture of the pig with her hobo stick.

Encourage play. Join the children as they pack the suitcases. If a child chooses to use the hobo stick, show her how to spread out the bandanna, put some clothes on it, then tie it on the stick. Encourage discussion.

Initiate travel play. Ask the children where they plan to go with their suitcases. How will they get there? Have them place chairs for a bus, plane, or train, and encourage them to pretend to travel on the bus (plane, train) to their destination.

Jamela's Dress
Day 2: Make-Believe Center

What to Do:

If you have the opportunity, elicit information about family celebrations prior to this activity. Expand the activity to include whatever customs are appropriate for the ethnicities represented in your classroom.

Relate the activity to the story. Remind the children that Jamela's mama was going to attend a wedding and that she needed something special to wear. Say that weddings are special, but that birthdays are very special days too. The person who is having the birthday is also special that day. They will have a pretend birthday party for the stuffed animal or doll.

Decide which toy is having a birthday. Show the toys to the children. Ask them which one they think is having a birthday today. Say that it is the smallest one and that it will be four years old! Let them compare the sizes of the toys to decide which one is the smallest.

Set up the birthday party. Have the children help decorate the area with the crepe paper, make other decorations if they choose to do so, wrap some pretend presents, and set the table for the birthday cake.

Have a celebration. Encourage the children to sing to the "birthday" toy, pretend to eat cake or whatever treat they have decided to have, and open the presents.

MATERIALS

- Party materials such as hats, crepe paper to decorate
- Stuffed animals or dolls
- Small boxes
- Wrapping paper
- Tape
- Table settings for party (plates, napkins, tableware, cups)

The Napping House
Day 1: Make-Believe Center

What to Do:

To prepare for the activity, inflate the balloons and draw the face of a character from the story on each balloon. Be sure to include a variety of colors of balloons, especially including those colors that individual children may need to learn. The balloons can also reinforce size relationships, with a fully inflated balloon representing the granny and a very slightly inflated one representing the flea.

Relate the activity to the story. Remind the children that all the characters got on top of each other on the bed and went to sleep. What happened to wake everyone up? Say that they will pretend that the parachute is the bed and they will put the balloon characters on the pretend bed.

Lift the parachute to waist height. Ask the children to help you spread the parachute flat on the floor. Have everyone stand around the parachute and hold the edge with both hands. Encourage the group to lift the parachute together to waist height.

Put one balloon on the parachute. Say, "Pretend the parachute is the bed in the story." Put a balloon on the parachute and say, "Let's pretend that this (red) balloon is the granny in the story. Granny is on the bed. Keep Granny on the bed!" Direct the group to move the parachute slowly up and down and from side to side, as you remind them to keep Granny on the bed. If the balloon falls off the parachute, ask the children to tell what happened to Granny.

Think of different ways to move the parachute. With one balloon on the parachute, encourage the children to think of other ways to move the parachute, such as by shaking their hands or walking around in a circle.

Place more balloons on the parachute, naming each character. Continue the activity with two or more balloons on the parachute, naming each balloon as a different character from the story. Also state the color of each balloon as you add it.

Pretend that the bed breaks. Put the balloons back on the parachute and suggest to the children that the bed is going to break, and all the characters will jump off. Have the children help you move the parachute up and down rapidly so that the balloons "jump off."

Review the activity. Sit with the children to discuss the activity. Which balloon stayed on the bed the longest? Which balloon fell off first?

MATERIALS

■ Parachute or old sheet
■ Bag of character balloons

The Snowy Day
Day 2: Make-Believe Center

What to Do:

Relate the activity to the story. Remind the children that Peter got dressed in very warm clothes and then went outside to play in the snow. Say that they will dress up and pretend to play in snow as Peter did.

Cover the floor with pretend snow. Give the children paper and show how to tear it up to make more snow. Have them sprinkle the shredded paper on the floor, as you talk about how they are covering the floor with pretend snow. As they work, state that real snow is very cold.

Dress up in winter clothes. Have the children choose dress-up clothes and pretend to get dressed for playing in the snow. Talk about the types of clothes they need for snow play, such as coats, hats, mittens, and scarves. Have them pretend to put on any items they do not have in the dress-up clothes.

Walk in pretend snow like Peter. Tell the children to pretend to go outdoors to look at the snow covering the ground. Then have them walk in the pretend snow as Peter did. Demonstrate some of the things Peter did in the snow for the children to try:

- Walk with toes pointing out.
- Walk with toes pointing in.
- Drag feet through the snow.
- Pretend to drag a stick in the snow.
- Make a pile of snow, like a snowman.
- Make snow angels.
- Make a snowball.

Move in other ways in the pretend snow. Put out the dolls, pretend sled, shovels, and other available props. Encourage the children to use the props to find more ways of moving around in the snow. Model some actions if the children need prompting:

- Pull dolls on pretend sleds.
- Shovel the snow into piles and sit in the piles.
- Roll around in the snow.
- Crumple together lots of paper to make a large ball.

As the children participate, ask questions that will promote conversation: "How did you make that big pile of snow? Tell Tina how you did that." "You covered the chair with snow. What else can you cover with snow?"

Remove outdoor clothes. After the children have played for a while, show how you go indoors and remove outdoor clothing to do indoor activities.

MATERIALS

- Some shredded paper (either white scrap paper or newspaper)
- Additional paper for children to tear apart for more snow
- Dress-up clothes or scraps of fabric (if possible, include such items as hats, scarves, mittens)
- Large heavy piece of cardboard with rope tied to one end, like a sled
- Dolls
- Other props for pretend snow play, such as shovels

Developmentally Appropriate Activities in Make-Believe

- Provide props that reflect experiences familiar to children—housekeeping, vehicles, doctor equipment. Young children use props realistically (brooms are for sweeping) and seldom expand. Allow and encourage older children to gather additional props for a particular role. Also encourage older children to substitute props, for example, using a bathroom-tissue tube as a microphone.

- Allow young children to use props near each other without interacting with each other. Encourage them to watch and imitate each other. Prompt older children to talk to each other, interact, and plan ideas together.

- Expect young children to take on very familiar roles, mainly those of adults at home. Older children can take on roles of other adults in the community. Suggest themes for dramatic play based on children's immediate experiences. For example, if there is a fire in the neighborhood, children will be very interested in pretending to be firefighters. They also enjoy pretending to be characters from familiar books and movies, as well as classroom visitors and people they have met on field trips.

- Ask open-ended questions to help children expand their play. "What else does a waitress do?" "How could the doctor help her feel better?"

- Join in play in order to model dramatic play techniques if needed. This is most appropriate when a child is ready for a more advanced level of play but needs encouragement. Also model how to interact with others or suggest ways for the child to interact: "Jose, help Lana feed the babies."

- Plan ahead what you will do if children act out sensitive issues such as drug abuse, violence, and sexual activity. Having a planned response allows you to handle the situation without making children feel guilty or frightened by your reaction. The best way to react is to join in and redirect the play. For example, if children are pretending to smoke, you might ask, "What else could we do?"

Spark Make-Believe Workshop

Teaching through Make-Believe

Teaching Strategies for Make-Believe

- Use positive reinforcement.

- Embed goals in activities.

- Be an enthusiastic, active participant.

- Teach through a blend of direct teaching and modeling.

- Encourage choices, exploration, experimentation, and problem solving.

Housekeeping

- Social: social interaction, increasing awareness of familiar family/community roles, following rules

- Language: conversational language

- Cognitive: sorting by category, one-to-one correspondence

Role-Play

- Social: learning to take another person's role, sharing materials

- Language: social conversation

- Cognitive: recall, building repertoire of experience

- Feelings: appropriate expression of emotions

Block Corner

- Cognition: matching shapes, predicting, problem solving, counting

- Social: sharing materials

- Language: talking to others

Vehicle Play

- Cognition: building repertoire of experience, increasing awareness of community, colors, counting, and big/little

- Language: conversational language

- Social: sharing materials

- Fine Motor: manipulating objects

Water-Table Play

- Social: social interaction, following rules

- Cognition: conservation (volume); science concepts such as wet/dry, absorption, sinking/floating, light/heavy

- Fine Motor: pouring, stirring

- Language: conversational language

Free-Play Activity

- What developmental skills were promoted when the children were in free play?

- How could the activity be adapted to meet the needs of children in your room?

- What else could you do with this activity?

Facilitated Free-Play Activity

- What developmental skills were promoted when an adult was facilitating free play?

- How could the activity be adapted to meet the needs of children in your room?

- What else could you do with this activity?

Spark Make-Believe Activity

- What developmental skills were promoted during the Spark activity?

- How could the activity be adapted to meet the needs of children in your room?

- What else could you do with this activity?

Spark Make-Believe

Spark Make-Believe activities are linked to the story of the week and the theme of the day.

Thinking through the Activity

- Did I ask questions during the activity?

- Did I try to promote child learning during the activity?

- Did I consider possible cultural differences?

- What could I have done better?

Promoting Language through Dramatic Play

- Comment on what children are doing.

- Introduce new vocabulary words.

- Use open-ended questions.

- Expand on what children say.

- Prompt children to talk to each other.

- Encourage children to use signs and labels.

Adult Involvement in Dramatic Play

Promotes social development when the adult encourages children to

- Get along with each other.

- Resolve conflicts.

- Express emotions of characters they act out.

Adult Involvement in Dramatic Play (Continued)

Promotes cognitive development when the adult encourages children to

■ Use language.

■ Solve problems.

■ Think creatively.

Promote Abstract Thinking

The adult can encourage abstract thinking by including

- Math

- Reading

- Social studies

- Charts, graphs, and maps

Developmentally Appropriate Make-Believe

- Preschool children should not be expected to act out an entire story.

- Preschool children may be able to role-play a single animal or character.

Summary

The intent of the Spark make-believe activities is to provide opportunities for teaching staff to promote general and individual skills of the children in their room.

WORKSHOP 4

Using Spark Activities: Music and Movement

I. Instructions for the Spark Trainer

II. Training Script

Introduction to Spark Music and Movement Center
Activities (15 minutes)

Activities That Are Meaningful to Children (10 minutes)

Exploring the Learning Potential of Music and
Movement Activities (45 minutes)

Learning to Teach and Adapt Spark Music and Movement
Activities (90 minutes)

Developing Skills (15 minutes)

Summary (5 minutes)

III. Handouts

IV. Overheads

I. Instructions for the Spark Trainer

Purpose

The purpose of the Music and Movement workshop is to help teachers learn how to implement the Spark music and movement center activities and to use these activities as a way to work on children's individual and general skills. They will learn teaching strategies to use to promote optimal learning during music center activities, consider ways to embed children's goals in activities, and discuss how to adapt activities to meet individual needs.

Preparing for the Workshop

This workshop is intended for no more than thirty people. Since all participants take part in the implementation of small-group activities and model an activity for the rest of the group, the process becomes tedious if too many activities are enacted. Therefore, if it is necessary to train more than thirty people simultaneously, ask a cofacilitator to work with half the group during the implementation of the Spark activities (see Learning to Teach and Adapt Spark Music and Movement Activities, page 188). This way, the large group may be divided into two segments, each of which then breaks into small groups and demonstrates their activities for their half of the large group. The workshop requires enough space for the participants to move around the room to music.

Note that in some cases this will be the third workshop based on activity centers, and that this one repeats some content from workshops 2 and 3. If you have already implemented the art and/or make-believe workshop, you may wish to skip some explanations, for example, how Child Goals handouts are used.

The following preparations will help make the workshop a success. Trainers should read through the instructions at least twice before starting to prepare for the workshop.

☐ Gather materials listed for the workshop.

☐ Prepare overheads.

☐ Set up overhead projector.

☐ Check the clarity of the first overhead on the overhead projector.

☐ Make copies of handouts.

☐ Set up the room for the first activity.

- ☐ Place materials needed for activities where you can reach them easily.
- ☐ Seat participants in teaching teams.
- ☐ Leave room at the front of the room for demonstrations.

Materials to Be Prepared and Gathered

- ☐ Overheads 401–427
- ☐ Timer to time activities (optional)
- ☐ Calculator to tally goals (optional)
- ☐ Cassette player and extension cord

For "Moving to Music" demonstration:

- ☐ Any commercial tape that is typically used in the classroom for movement

For Spark "Music and Movement" demonstration:

- ☐ Recording of happy-sounding music with a strong beat
- ☐ Four slide whistles or kazoos
- ☐ Eight jingle bells of varying sizes
- ☐ Drum or tambourine

Materials for music centers in the following Spark units:

- ☐ *Chicka Chicka Boom Boom*, day 3
- ☐ *If You Give a Pig a Pancake*, day 1
- ☐ *The Little Mouse, the Red Ripe Strawberry and the Big Hungry Bear*, day 2
- ☐ *The Napping House*, day 4
- ☐ *No Fair to Tigers*, day 1

Spark Books

- ☐ *Chicka Chicka Boom Boom*
- ☐ *If You Give a Pig a Pancake*
- ☐ *The Little Mouse, the Red Ripe Strawberry, and the Big Hungry Bear*
- ☐ *The Napping House*
- ☐ *No Fair to Tigers*

Handouts

☐   One copy each of the following Spark Activity sheets:

☐   *Chicka Chicka Boom Boom,* Day 3, Music and Movement

☐   *If You Give a Pig a Pancake,* Day 1, Music and Movement

☐   *The Little Mouse, the Red Ripe Strawberry, and the Big Hungry Bear,* Day 2, Music and Movement

☐   *The Napping House,* Day 4, Music and Movement

☐   *No Fair to Tigers,* Day 1, Music and Movement

☐   You Can Teach Music

☐   Child Goals, six for each participant (see appendix 2)

II. Training Script

Introduction to Spark Music and Movement Center Activities

As the participants gather, display overhead 401.

Review of the Spark Teaching Strategies

Show OH 401, Spark Music Workshop.

Talk about the suggested strategies for teaching the Spark music and movement center. Stress the fact that they are the same strategies used to teach all other Spark center activities.

Show OH 402, Teaching Strategies for Music Activities.

The Challenge of Music

Ask how participants feel about music. **Show OH 403,** Plato, **OH 404,** Impact on Preliteracy, **OH 405,** Validating Many Cultures, and **OH 406,** Receptive Prekindergartners.

Ask participants how they feel about teaching through music. Do they think that children can learn through music, or do they use music as a way to entertain children between planned activities? Suggest that music is one of the most effective teaching tools available to them. Say that through the ages, people have recognized the impact that music has on them. Show overheads 403 and 404 and say that music is especially effective when used appropriately in preschool classrooms. Show and talk about overheads 405 and 406.

Show OH 407, Spark Music. Discuss difficulties with teaching music.

Say that like story reading, art, and make-believe, music is an activity that young children find highly engaging; therefore, music activities are another teaching tool used by the Spark curriculum. Show overhead 407 and say that music is more challenging than art and make-believe because many teachers are intimidated by music. Ask how many people think they can't sing. Ask for a show of hands. Say that children don't care how you sing—they think their teachers can do anything! The important thing when teaching music activities is to be enthusiastic and to enjoy the activity with the children.

Use overhead 408 to discuss workshop goals.

Show OH 408, Goals of the Workshop; discuss.

Activities That Are Meaningful to Children

Music in the Preschool Classroom

Talk about the fact that typical early childhood classrooms use music activities because most children are highly interested in music. They like to move, they like to play instruments, they like to experiment with sound, and they like to sing.

Summarize by saying that if the teaching staff show that they like and enjoy music, the children's natural love of music will come through.

Show OH 409, Children Like To . . . .

Relate Music Activities to Participants' Experience

Ask if anyone uses music in the classroom and model holding up your hand. Discuss the types of music activities that the participants already use in their classrooms. Write their responses on a blank transparency. After all suggestions have been recorded, say that these are all good ways to use music in the classroom.

Use blank transparency to list how participants use music.

Exploring the Learning Potential of Music and Movement Activities

Demonstration: Singing Songs

State that there are many developmental goals that may be promoted during music activities. Participants will watch demonstrations of different approaches to see how many of the goals are addressed. Show a sample Child Goals handout and say that they have enough copies for all of the demonstrations that they will see. Discuss the handout, explaining that it contains developmental goals listed under each of the five domains. Say that as they watch the demonstrations, they should circle any goals on the sheet that they see being addressed. Stress that they should circle only goals that are actually promoted, not ones that could be promoted, during the activity. At the end of each activity, they will count the goals they circled and put the number at the upper-right corner of their paper.

Introduce Child Goals handout.

Ask for three volunteers to pretend to be preschool children. Tell the other participants to mark their Child Goals handouts as they observe the activity.

Ask for volunteers. Ask others to mark Child Goals handouts.

Conduct "Singing Songs" demonstration, tally goals, and record. Show OH 410, "Singing Songs" Demonstration.

Sit on the floor with the volunteers and sing a song. Use a simple song that you know is typically used in the classrooms. Sing it through twice, just as teachers do with children in the classroom. Ask the volunteers to sing the song with you. Thank the volunteers for singing with you. Tally the goals and record them on a blank transparency, then use overhead 410 to discuss the learning potential of the activity.

Demonstration: Moving to Music

Say that you would like all participants to pretend to be children, and that they don't need to mark the Child Goal handouts. Ask them to stand and move to an area where there is enough room for movement. Play some music that is commonly used in classrooms for movement.

Conduct "Moving to Music" demonstration.

In your role as "teacher," join the "children" as they move to the music. Show enthusiasm, but don't teach during the activity. After approximately five minutes, turn off the tape and thank participants for their participation. Ask them to return to their seats.

Show OH 411, "Moving to Music" Demonstration; discuss cultural differences.

Use overhead 411 to discuss the demonstration. Make it clear that the recorded music cannot be adapted to meet the needs of individual children. Remind them that children may react differently to music depending on their cultural backgrounds. Brainstorm how to respond to the differences.

Demonstration: Spark Music and Movement Activity

Say that the next part of the activity is a Spark music center activity from the *Napping House* unit. Briefly review the story and the concepts of the week: *on/off, falling down, counting,* and *happy.* Say that the activity they are going to do is the day 4 music and movement activity based on the concept *happy.*

Review *Napping House* story and concepts; day 4, *happy.*

Ask for three volunteers. Ask the remaining participants to circle goals that they see promoted on their Child Goals handouts. Go to an area where there is room for movement. Sit on the floor with the "children."

Ask for volunteers, tell observers to mark Child Goals handouts.

Conduct the *Napping House* day 4 music and movement activity, following the curriculum page. Join in the activity with the "children," relating the activity to the story, encouraging creativity, modeling behavior, encouraging choices, asking questions, and providing positive reinforcement. Be sure to include such questions as the following in the discussion:

Conduct *Napping House* day 4 music and movement activity.

▪ Why are the people in the story happy at the end?

▪ What color are the jingle bells, the kazoos, and the slide whistles?

- If you have both slide whistles and kazoos, which is longer, the kazoo or the slide whistle?

- Discuss the size relationship of the jingle bells—are they big or are they little?

- What shape are the jingle bells?

- How many jingle bells is (name) playing (if child plays more than one)?

Thank the volunteers and ask them to return to their seats.

Tally goals and record. Compare the number of goals promoted during the Spark activity to the goals promoted during the song. Use overhead 412 to guide a discussion of the activity.

Show OH 412, Spark Music and Movement Activity; discuss. **Show OH 413, 414,** and **415,** Spark Activity Skills.

With overheads 413, 414, and 415 displayed, talk about the developmental skills that were promoted during the Spark music activity, including gross and fine motor; cognitive; and language, social, and creative.

Summarize the Demonstrations

Say that the demonstrations have compared different ways of using music activities in the preschool classroom. Stress that all three uses of music are valid and should be used. Use overheads 416, 417, and 418 to point out the skills that can be promoted in each type of activity. Talk about the fact that Spark combines all the elements of music activities and also encourages experimentation and exploration.

Show OH 416, 417, and **418.** Discuss.

Developmentally Appropriate Music

With overhead 419 displayed, ask the participants to raise their hands if they have had training in developmentally appropriate art activities for young children prior to these workshops. Ask if they have had training in the levels of play (including drama or make-believe). Now ask how many have had training in developmentally appropriate music activities for preschool children. State that music activities, just like all other activities, must be developmentally appropriate to be effective in promoting learning in young children, but that most teachers haven't had this kind of training in music.

Show OH 419, ask participants about training.

With overhead 420 displayed, discuss *tempo* as follows: Recorded music for young children is often not recorded at an appropriate tempo. Both songs and movement tapes may move too quickly for young children. *Songs* need to be adjusted to the speed at which a young child is able to articulate the words. *Movement* needs to be adjusted to a tempo at which children can

Show OH 420, Developmentally Appropriate Music: Tempo.

control their muscles. For example, a marching tempo must be a comfortable walking pace. If you are encouraging young children to move to a drumbeat, observe them carefully, and adjust the beat to their ability. State that the major problem with commercially recorded music, both songs and music for movement, is that it often cannot be adapted to meet children's needs.

Show OH 421, Developmentally Appropriate Music: Range and Repetition.

With overhead 421 displayed, discuss *range* and *repetition* as follows: Young children typically have a very limited range in which they can sing (middle C to the F above middle C). Songs should not have wide skips in the melody, but should concentrate instead on a few notes in this limited range. Most folk songs fit this criterion, for example, "Old MacDonald," "Skip to My Lou," and "Mary Had a Little Lamb." If a teacher starts a song that children know but the children aren't singing along, the teacher should sing the song a little lower or a little higher. The range that is comfortable for most women is also comfortable for most children.

Count melodic phrases in "Mary Had a Little Lamb."
Show OH 422, Developmentally Appropriate Songs.

Repeating musical phrases is also developmentally appropriate. Most three- and four-year-old children are inexperienced singers. They need an opportunity to practice singing simple musical phrases in order to become successful singers. For this reason, the less complex a song is, the more successfully they will be able to sing it. Songs that preschool children enjoy singing have the same phrase repeated often, such as "Mary Had a Little Lamb." Point out how often the same melodic phrase is used in this song.

Show OH 423, Skip to My Lou.

Successful songs for preschoolers also have repeated word patterns. Learning to sing is a complicated task; using songs with repeated words simplifies the task. Again, folk songs contain many repeated words. With overhead 423 showing, point out the repeated word patterns in "Skip to My Lou." Say that children love singing and will not be harmed by singing songs that do not follow these criteria. However, it is easier for them to sing if these types of songs are used.

Say that the Spark activities have been carefully developed to ensure that they are developmentally appropriate for preschool children.

Learning to Teach and Adapt Spark Music and Movement Activities

Team Demonstration

Show OH 424, Teaching a Spark Music Activity; distribute music and movement activities to teams.

Review the stories *The Little Mouse, the Red Ripe Strawberry, and the Big Hungry Bear; If You Give a Pig a Pancake; No Fair to Tigers;* and

Chicka Chicka Boom Boom with the group. Break the group into teams of no more than seven people, and give each team one of the four Spark music activities you prepared. Tell them that they will have fifteen minutes to read through the activity, decide how they want to present it to the group, and gather and prepare the materials. Tell them where to find the materials. Say that when they present the activity to the group, they should first tell everyone what unit their activity was drawn from and what the concept of their day is. This will strengthen the activity and give it meaning.

As each group works, go from team to team, giving help as needed. Tell them to select a teacher for the activity, decide what developmental goals they will promote, and rehearse the activity. After a reasonable amount of time has passed and the groups are prepared, assemble the large group and ask a team to volunteer to be first. Remind observers to mark Child Goals handouts.

Encourage each team to lead its activity while the other participants observe and mark their handouts. Lead a round of applause as each team finishes its activity.

Tally goal sheets. Use overhead 425 to discuss the team presentations.

Compliment the teaching teams for doing an excellent job. Say that no two activities would have the same number of child goals embedded in the activity, but all of the teams promoted many goals. Read the average scores of each team's activity to reinforce the impact that Spark activities have on child growth.

Developing Skills

Learning Rhymes

Remind the participants that spoken rhymes also help develop preliteracy skills. For this reason, there are rhymes in the Spark units; some are called "raps." Say that although rhymes are not music, they can have a rhythmic beat and should be chanted rhythmically. State that the teacher should learn a rhyme in advance and continue to use it whenever appropriate. The more rhymes are used in the classroom, the more effective their impact on preliteracy.

Use overhead 426 to teach "City Rap," encouraging participants to clap on the beat and chant together until everyone seems comfortable. It may help to clap four slow, evenly spaced beats, then start the chant. The words "If you" should precede the first clap.

Help teams prepare.

Have participants present; lead applause.

Tally goal sheets. Show OH 425, Thinking through the Activity; discuss.

Compliment teams. Report scores.

Show OH 426, City Rap, teach rap, encourage clapping and chanting.

Show OH 427, Choose a
Rhythm, model rhythms, have
participants clap.

Moving to a Drumbeat

State that since it may be difficult to find recorded music with appropriate tempos for young children, an excellent way to provide rhythms is to beat a drum.

With overhead 427 showing, model each of the rhythms by playing it on a large drum or tambourine. Have the group clap along with you. Practice each rhythm until the group can clap it successfully.

Summary

Write teaching strategies on
blank transparency.

Remind the participants again that the teaching strategies suggested for use in the Spark curriculum are the same throughout all segments of the curriculum, including storytelling time and art, make-believe, and music centers. Review the strategies; write each on a blank transparency and review it before moving on to the next:

- Offer positive reinforcement.

- Encourage active participation.

- Ask questions.

- Embed goals.

- Encourage choices.

- Use a blend of direct teaching and modeling.

- Avoid having children wait.

- Demonstrate enthusiasm.

Stress that one of the most important things to do is to prepare, prepare, prepare!

Refer to handout, You Can
Teach Music.

State that music, art, and make-believe activities are much more than singing songs, drawing pictures, and playing in the housekeeping or block corner. These activities are highly interesting to children and therefore are important teaching vehicles. Say that they have a handout titled "You Can Teach Music" that will give them additional suggestions for using music in their classrooms. Remind them that it isn't necessary to be a great artist, singer, or actor to teach through the arts. Anyone can teach through art, music, and make-believe.

Chicka Chicka Boom Boom
Day 3: Music and Movement Center

What to Do:

In advance, prepare the letters that are most appropriate for your group of children by printing a pair of letters on a piece of paper, then cutting the paper in half so that a letter is displayed on each half-sheet. If the group is young, prepare two matching letters (*A A*). If the children are older, prepare a lowercase letter and its matching uppercase letter.

Relate the activity to the story. Remind the children that when the little letters fell out of the tree, the mamas and papas and uncles and aunts all came running to help. Families like to help each other. They will pretend that two of them are in the same letter family and they will do things together.

Distribute the letters and tape on the children. Sit with the children on the floor. Spread the letter pairs out. (If the group is older, scramble the letters and encourage the children to pair the lowercase and uppercase letters.) Give a letter to each child and tape it to his chest. Stress the name of the letter. Help the children find their partners (the other child with the same letter).

Start mirror movements. With one child, show the others how to be "mirrors." Stand facing each other, place the palms of your hands together, and say that you are the "papa" and the "child" should do exactly what you do. Model simple movements until you are sure the children understand the activity. Ask the children to stand, facing each other. For older children, have the child with the uppercase letter be the leader first. For younger children, designate the pair leader. Encourage them to start mirror movement. After a while, change leaders. (If the group includes a nonambulatory child, the activity can be done with the children sitting, facing each other.)

Move to music. Ask the children to move to music, holding hands with their partner. Stress that families work and play together.

Sing a song. Have the children sit again; say that families have fun together. To the tune of "If You're Happy and You Know It," sing:

> *If you're having fun, sing with me*
> *If you're having fun, sing with me*
> *If you're having fun, we'll get a whole lot done,*
> *If you're having fun, sing with me.*

MATERIALS

- Set of lowercase letters
- Set of uppercase letters
- Masking tape
- Cassette player
- Tape of music

If You Give a Pig a Pancake
Day 1: Music and Movement Center

What to Do:

Prepare circles that will promote the skill development of each individual child.

MATERIALS
■ Brown circles, cut in half, with a shape, color, or numeral on each half

Relate the activity to the story. Sit in a circle on the floor with the children. Remind them that the girl in the story shared her breakfast pancakes with a pig. Say that they will pretend that they are pancake pigs.

Teach a song. Sing the Pancake Pig song through several times to the tune of "Oh, Do You Know the Muffin Man," encouraging the children to join you as they become familiar with the song.

> *Do you know the pancake pig,*
> *The pancake pig, the pancake pig,*
> *Do you know the pancake pig*
> *Who came to visit me?*

Distribute the circle halves. Give each child one half of a paper pancake. Distribute them according to the skill level of the child. (Some children may need to learn shapes, others colors, and some may be ready to identify numerals.) Tell them to put their pancakes on the floor in front of them.

Sing the Pancake Pig song. Match similar shapes, colors, or numerals. Tell the children to help you sing and that when you sing about their pancake, they should hold it up and say "Yes!" For example, sing, "Do you know the two pig...," or "Do you know the rectangle pig..." When the child says "Yes," give her the other half and encourage her to put her pancake together. When all the children have complete circles with matching halves, tell them that now they are all pancake pigs!

Move to the Pancake Pig song. Collect the pancakes (or tape half of the pancake on the child) and ask the children to stand. Remind the children that the pig in the book liked to dance. (If necessary, show them the picture in the book.) Start singing, "Can you dance like the pancake pig, the pancake pig, the pancake pig," and encourage the children to show you how the pancake pig danced.

Ask the children what else the pancake pig did when she visited the girl. If necessary, look through the book with them. Act upon each of the children's suggestions by inserting the action in the song and encouraging the children to act out the action in any way they choose. (For example, Can you build like the pancake pig? Can you eat like the pancake pig? Can you wash like the pancake pig? And so on.)

The Little Mouse, the Red Ripe Strawberry, and the Big Hungry Bear
Day 2: Music and Movement Center

What to Do:

MATERIALS

- Floor shapes (red, green, blue, yellow)
- Cassette player
- Recorded marching music

Consider the individual goals of the children in your classroom as you choose colors and shapes for this activity. You might want to put chalk marks on the floor to guide children in placing their shapes with enough room to march around them.

Relate the activity to the story. Ask the children if they remember how the mouse guarded the strawberry. What was he holding when he was guarding it? Why would he hold a key? Encourage them to realize that the chain around the strawberry has a lock and that the key would unlock the lock. Ask them what else they see on the floor around the strawberry (thumbtacks). Remind them that they are going to pretend to be the mouse guarding the strawberry, but they will guard shapes instead of strawberries.

Identify and place shapes. Show each shape. Ask the children to identify the color and shape of each one. Encourage each child to choose a shape and to place the shape on the floor.

Explain the game. Say that you are going to start the music and that they should march around the shapes like the mouse until the music stops. When the music stops, they should sit on the closest shape. The first time through, lead the line. Weave around all the shapes; demonstrate marching like the mouse guarding the strawberry.

Continue the activity, encouraging a child to be the line leader. Repeat as long as the children are interested in the activity.

Close the activity by singing the following words to the tune of "Skip to My Lou."

> *Red, red, who's wearing red?*
> *Red, red, who's wearing red?*
> *Red, red, who's wearing red?*
> *Stand up if you're wearing red!*
>
> *(repeat, changing colors)*

The Napping House
Day 4: Music and Movement Center

What to Do:

Relate the activity to the story. Remind the children that even though the bed broke and everyone fell down, all the characters were happy at the end of the story. Say that when people are happy they often make some kind of a happy sound. Encourage a discussion of what they like to do when they are happy.

Make happy sounds with slide whistles. Invite the children to find the slide whistle or kazoo that has their name on it. Show how you can make happy sounds with your slide whistle or kazoo. Encourage them to experiment to create different sounds. To prompt them you might make a sound and ask if anyone can make another happy sound.

Take turns making happy sounds as you sing a song. Ask the children to sit in a circle with their slide whistles behind their backs. Then to the tune of, "Mary Had a Little Lamb," sing the following in a cheerful manner:

> We are making happy sounds,
> Happy sounds, happy sounds.
> We are making happy sounds,
> Happy sounds today.

Then point to one child and ask her to make a happy sound with her slide whistle or kazoo. After the child makes the sound, ask if it made everyone feel happy. Encourage discussion. Then repeat the song and point to another child to make a happy sound. Continue this procedure until every child has had a turn to play a happy sound. As each child finishes playing her instrument, have her put it behind her back.

Make happy sounds with jingle bells. Collect the slide whistles. Tell them they can make more happy sounds with other instruments. Shake the jingle bells and ask them if you made a happy sound. Ask what the bells make them think of. (Older children might respond, "Christmas.") Let them experiment with the bells and then repeat the above song with the bells.

Play music for movement and instrumental accompaniment. Play the tape through and encourage the children to play their happy instruments or to get up and move to the music. Encourage creative movement, complimenting children who move in different ways.

Close the activity by singing "If You're Happy." Sit with the children to sing "If You're Happy and You Know It." Lead movements to go with various verses:

> If you're happy and you know it
> touch your nose   lie down low
> touch your ear   nod your head
> jump up high   blink your eyes

MATERIALS

- Cassette player
- Recording of happy music
- Slide whistles or kazoos
- Jingle bells

No Fair to Tigers

Day 1: Music and Movement Center

What to Do:

MATERIALS

- Strips of construction paper (orange, black, and white)
- Orange, black, and white streamers
- Cassette player
- Recorded music appropriate for moving

Relate the activity to the story. Ask the children what color Old Tiger was. Help them to remember that he was orange, black, and white. Have them look at their clothing and then label the target colors by asking if anyone is wearing orange. Is anyone wearing black? white? Remind them that first they will sing a song and then move to music with streamers.

Distribute strips of colored construction paper. Spread the colors out on the floor. Let each child choose a color strip to hold. Ask all the children that are holding orange to hold it high. Repeat with each color until you are sure the children know what color they are holding. Ask the children to stand.

Sing a color song. Sing the following song, using the tune from "If You're Happy and You Know It." Encourage the children to follow the directions when their color is mentioned in the song. Ask the children who are not holding the specified color to help you sing as they become acquainted with the song.

If your color's black, turn around	*If your color's orange, jump up high*	*If your color's white, touch the ground*
If your color's black, turn around	*If your color's orange, jump up high*	*If your color's white, touch the ground*
If it's black and you know it	*If it's orange and you know it*	*If it's white and you know it*
Then your turn will surely show it	*Then your jump will surely show it*	*Then your touch will surely show it*
If your color's black, turn around!	*If your color's orange, jump up high!*	*If your color's white, touch the ground!*

Encourage the children to trade colors, then sing the song again. Trade colors one more time to ensure that everyone has an opportunity to identify each color by his response to the sung directions. Praise the children for good listening.

Sit with the children and distribute streamers. Ask the children to give you their color strips. Then have each child choose and label the colors of one or two streamers.

Move with the music. Start the music and join the children as they move to the music with the streamers. As you move, comment on what you and the children are doing: "Joshua is holding his orange streamer up high!" "Maria is going around and around with her black streamer!" "I'm moving my streamers up and down."

Sing a new verse. Quiet the children by singing the following verse to the previous song about colors as the children sit on the floor with you.

If you had fun say hurrah! (Hurrah!)
If you had fun say hurrah! (Hurrah!)
If it was fun and you know it,
Then your face will surely show it
If you had fun, say hurrah! (Hurrah!)

You Can Teach Music

■ Show that you are comfortable with music and enjoy it. Make music an integral part of the program: (1) sing the Spark songs at other times of the day; (2) place instruments in the music center to enable children to experiment with sound during free play; (3) reinforce children's original songs that may be sung during other times of the day by saying such things as, "Nice song. I like the way you are singing"; (4) reinforce creative movement whenever it may occur.

■ During the Spark hour, take time during the group activity to tell what will be done at the music center. Present it in an enticing manner. Show by your tone of voice and attitude that *you* think the activity will be fun!

■ Review the intent of the activity by sitting with the children to discuss the activity before you begin. This will focus attention on the concept that is being introduced and make the learning experience meaningful.

■ Adapt the activity to the level of the group. If necessary, add concrete objects such as plastic animals or other objects. Include colors, shapes, and body parts that individual children need to learn. If children have disabilities, encourage them to participate according to their ability levels.

■ Introduce new musical instruments one at a time. Talk about each instrument and mention its name. Draw attention to its shape, color, and sound. Let the children take turns playing it. If the instrument is fragile, discuss its limitations and ask the children for suggestions as to how it should be handled. If the instrument is not fragile, place it in the music and movement center to let the children experiment with the sound.

■ Lose your inhibitions and show enjoyment. Show the children by your attitude that you enjoy music and are glad to be taking part in the activity. Smile, move to the beat, take part in movement, and be dramatic. No matter how you sing, move, or play an instrument, the children will think your skills are superior.

■ Accept and reinforce the children's creativity. Accept the children's ideas. Encourage them to experiment with instruments, movement, and songs. Find something good to say about each child's movement. Encourage the children to move in the way they choose as long as the movement is appropriate.

■ Accept and reinforce the children's unique songs as you would a child's created story.

■ Invite a child to sit or stand with you if the child's response is inappropriate. If children are running wildly instead of marching to the beat, focus their listening skills by having them clap to the beat. After they seem to recognize what type of movement is appropriate, encourage them to rejoin the other children. If a child is reluctant to move, encourage the child to play an instrument to accompany the taped music.

■ Play all types of music in your classroom: jazz, classical, popular, Dixieland, blues, and music from other countries. Provide children with the opportunities to enjoy and move to many different types of music.

Spark Music Workshop

Teaching through Music

Teaching Strategies for Music Activities

- Use positive reinforcement.

- Embed general and individual goals in activities.

- Be an enthusiastic, active participant.

- Teach through a blend of modeling and direct teaching.

- Encourage choices, exploration, experimentation, and problem solving.

- Ask both open-ended and closed questions.

Plato

Plato considered music to be the most potent of the arts because it reaches to the soul and imparts grace.

Impact on Preliteracy

Songs, poems, and games that emphasize rhyming or manipulation of sound increase children's phonological awareness and are valuable preliteracy activities.

(Taken from Preschool-Specific Recommendations for State Leadership Excerpts from *Preventing Reading Difficulties in Young Children*, National Research Council, 1998. C. E. Snow, M. S. Burns, and P. Griffin, eds., Washington, D.C.: National Academy Press).

Validating Many Cultures

Using music from many cultures validates
the heritage of each child in the classroom.

Receptive Prekindergartners

"If pre-kindergartners are receptive to all types of music, what better time than early childhood to introduce them to a wide variety of world music?"

Ellen McCullough-Brabson, 1992

Spark Music

- Music is an integral part of the curriculum.

- Music activities are used to promote child growth.

Goals of the Workshop

- To understand the impact of music experiences on a child's development.

- To understand what types of music activities are developmentally appropriate for young children.

- To understand how music can contribute to a child's acceptance of differences.

- To develop experience in implementing music activities.

Children Like To . . .

- Move

- Play instruments

- Experiment with sound

- Sing

"Singing Songs" Demonstration

- What developmental skills were promoted?

- How could the song be adapted to meet the needs of individual children?

- What else could you do with this song?

"Moving to Music" Demonstration

- What developmental skills were promoted during this activity?

- How could the recorded music be adapted to meet the needs of individual children?

- What else could you do with this activity?

Spark Music and Movement Activity

■ What developmental skills were promoted during this activity?

■ How could you adapt this activity for individual children in your class?

■ What else could you do with this activity?

Spark Activity Skills (1)
Gross Motor, Fine Motor

Gross Motor:

- Move to rhythmic beat

- Move different body parts

- Imitate movements of others

- Jump

Fine Motor:

- Play musical instruments to rhythmic beat

- Manipulate objects with motor control

- Rotate wrist to manipulate objects

- Imitate hand motions

Spark Activity Skills (2) Cognitive

- Gain in understanding of body part labels

- Follow directions

- Gain understanding of concept *happy*

- Recall words to song

- Show understanding of size relationships

- Compare attributes

Spark Activity Skills (3) Language, Social, Creative

Language:

- Answer questions
- Participate in group song
- Share information
- Show understanding of positional words
- Answer yes or no appropriately

Social:

- Share materials
- Join in group activity
- Follow simple rules
- Take turns
- Experiment appropriately with class-room materials

Creative:

- Choose how to respond to music/beat
- Choose how to make musical sound

Promoting Skills: Singing Songs

- Social: participation in group activity

- Language: articulation, increasing vocabulary

- Cognitive: recall, showing awareness of shapes, colors, body parts, sequencing

- Fine Motor: hand motions

- Gross Motor: moving to a beat

Promoting Skills: Moving to Music

- Social: participation in group activity

- Language: labeling actions, body parts, colors, shapes

- Cognitive: solving problems, spatial relationships, creative thinking, identify body parts, shapes, colors

- Gross motor: moving to beat

Promoting Skills: Exploring Sounds

- Social: sharing materials, following directions, listening

- Language: answering questions, labeling, conversational language

- Cognitive: problem solving, showing awareness of size relationships, sorting

- Fine Motor: pincer grasp, opening/closing containers

Developmentally Appropriate Music

Many skills can be taught through music, but the music used needs to be developmentally appropriate.

Developmentally Appropriate Music: Tempo

Tempo (speed) of the recording for movement

■ Is it too fast or too slow?

Tempo (speed) of the song

■ Is it at the right speed for the children's speech, articulation, and understanding?

Developmentally Appropriate Music: Range and Repetition

Range of the song

- Is it too high or too low for the children to sing?

Repetition

- Does the song have repeated musical phrases?

- Does the song have repeated words?

Developmentally Appropriate Songs

Learning to sing is a complicated task.

- Repeated words,

- Repeated musical phrases, and

- A small range of musical pitches make the task easier.

Skip to My Lou

Skip, skip, skip to my Lou,

Skip, skip, skip to my Lou,

Skip, skip, skip to my Lou,

Skip to my Lou, my darling.

Teaching a Spark Music Activity

- Notice what the concept of the day is for your activity. Be able to tell the group.

- Choose a leader to be the teacher.

- Make needed preparations.

- Decide what child goals to promote.

- Run through the activity.

Thinking through the Activity

- Did I ask questions?

- Did I promote child growth?

- Did I consider possible cultural differences?

- How could I have done better?

City Rap

If you live in a city and you like to walk,

You can walk with your momma and talk and talk.

First you walk fast, and then you walk slow,

Then puff out your cheeks and blow and blow.

Stop when you're ready to cross the street,

Look both ways, then move your feet!

Choose a Rhythm

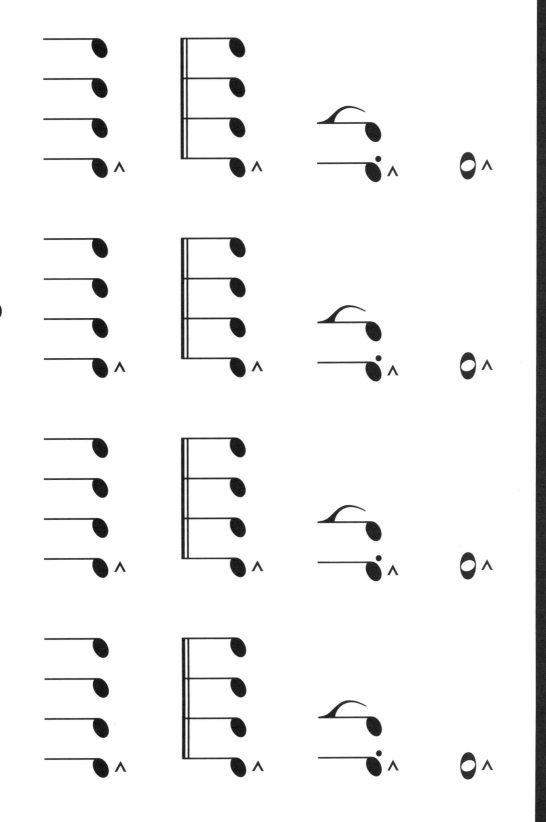

WORKSHOP 5

Evaluation and Further Training

I. Instructions for the Spark Trainer

II. Training Script

Introduction to Evaluating the Spark Program

Using the Observation Checklist (30 minutes)

Using the Child Goals Handout (15 minutes)

Using the Teacher Evaluation Form (15 minutes)

Using the Spark Parent Evaluation Form (15 minutes)

Summary (10 minutes)

III. Handouts (see appendix 1)

I. Instructions for the Spark Trainer

Purpose

The purpose of the Evaluation and Further Training workshop is to help administrators learn how to use the Spark evaluation forms to determine the impact of the Spark curriculum on their program.

Preparing for the Workshop

The following preparations will help make the workshop a success:

☐ Read through the instructions at least twice before starting to prepare for the workshop.

☐ Make a copy of each of the evaluation forms for each participant. The forms can be found in appendix 1.

II. Training Script

Introduction to Evaluating the Spark Program

Program administrators can evaluate the effectiveness of the Spark curriculum in their early childhood programs by using several tools. The best way to find out how well Spark is working within the program is to ask—ask the parents, ask the staff, and make independent observations. This workshop presents tools to collect, organize, and evaluate information from those sources and to apply the results toward future staff training.

Four tools will help program managers or other administrators assess how well the Spark curriculum is working and what aspects of the curriculum are perceived as either positive or negative. The Observation Checklist and the Child Goals handout show how well the teacher implements the curriculum, promotes goals, and uses suggested teaching strategies in the classroom. The Spark Teacher Evaluation form records a teacher's perception of the curriculum. The Spark Parent Evaluation form gathers feedback from parents. The use of each of these forms will be discussed in the following sections.

Introduce four evaluation tools: the Observation Checklist; the Child Goals chart; the Teacher Evaluation form; and the Parent Evaluation form.

Using the Observation Checklist

State that the way a curriculum is implemented in classrooms may determine whether the curriculum is a success or a failure in pro-

Say that to be effective, Spark must be used as designed.

moting child growth. If the Spark curriculum is not implemented as intended, if the story is not read every day, if the teacher does not use activities that are developed on the theme of the day, and if she does not enable the children to participate in multisensory learning by using at least two center activities a day, then children cannot be expected to benefit from the Spark curriculum.

Say that the Observation Checklist is a form that program directors, supervisors, or administrators can use to determine the fidelity and level of implementation of the Spark curriculum in the classroom. It is a tool for them to use during classroom observations to rate how well the teacher is using the teaching strategies suggested during the Spark in-service training and implementing the Spark activities. Say that the form includes questions and a yes/no check-off answer sheet to guide their attention to specific implementation aspects that indicate how closely teachers are following the curriculum. Distribute and talk through the Observation Checklist. Point out that the form includes a place to enter identification information about the classrooms, definitions of the terms used in the form, and observation checklists for the large-group story-reading activity, and for two small-group center activities.

Suggest that the checklist is most effective when it is used at least twice during the year, once in the fall, and once in the spring. Suggest that they should make the first observation approximately a month after the in-service training and say that teachers will appreciate having a month to become familiar with the curriculum before they are observed. The initial observations will enable administrators to determine how well the teachers understand the curriculum and whether they are using the strategies that have been recommended during in-service training.

Say that it is critical to have a conference with each teaching team following the observation to provide feedback to the teachers. During this conference the administrator should go over the Observation Checklist form with the teaching team and discuss what they are doing well and areas in which they may need to improve.

Say that the second observation is often most effective when it is made in the spring after teachers have been implementing the curriculum for several months. This observation will enable the administrator to determine the teachers' growth in the use of the suggested teaching strategies, ability to adapt activities to promote both general and individual child goals, and implementation of the curriculum.

Distribute Observation Checklist, discuss.

Describe observation and conference timing, fall and spring.

Describe expectations for first observation.

State that the first observation in the first year that teachers implement the Spark activities may reveal that they are implementing the activities as written but are not adapting activities for individual children, promoting individual child goals, asking open-ended questions, or using specific reinforcement. Say that this is typical of early implementation. Change is difficult. Say that the Spark curriculum encourages teachers to use a different approach, to use unfamiliar stories, and to implement new curricular activities. The combination of so many different things is difficult to master. Stress that during this period the teaching staff will need the administrator's support and encouragement. The most successful programs are the ones in which the teachers receive strong administrative support.

Describe expectations for second and subsequent observations.

Say that by the end of the year, most teachers are using many of the suggested teaching strategies and are beginning to adapt the activities to meet the needs of individual children in their classes. State that teachers who have used Spark have indicated that after they master the strategies and become familiar with the curriculum, they find it simple and fun to use. Second-year Spark teachers are often eager to help with in-service training and become mentors for new teachers.

Describe observation scheduling concerns and preparation.

Remind them that each day of a Spark unit takes approximately an hour to implement, so the administrator will need to schedule an hour for the observation. After a story-reading segment that takes approximately half an hour, the teachers and their assistants will implement two center activities simultaneously. Each of the center activities is gone through twice, so that all the children have an opportunity to participate in each activity and participate in multisensory learning. Since day 5 of each unit follows a simplified format, they should avoid scheduling on that day (usually a Friday). State that when they set up the observation, they should ask the teachers which unit and day's activities will be implemented during the observation so that they can become familiar with the activities ahead of time; several questions on the checklist require that the observer be knowledgeable about the activities. Say that it is important for them to be in the room before the story begins and to stay to observe two center/small-group activities.

Explain Checklist definitions, marking; ask if there are questions.

Say that the definitions of terms used on the checklist will help them decide about such issues as open-ended versus closed questions. During the observation, they should tally the numbers of open-ended or closed questions and positive feedback responses to the child that the teacher uses, then circle the appropriate number. This will provide accurate feedback for the conference they have with the teacher following the observation. Ask participants if they have questions about the checklist.

Say that teachers can use the Observation Checklist too, as a self-evaluation tool. This use of the checklist enables them to reflect upon their implementation of the Spark curriculum and their use of suggested teaching strategies.

Explain teacher use for self-evaluation.

Using the Child Goals Handout

Say that in addition to the Observation Checklist, administrators may use the Child Goals chart during observations of the small-group center activities. Distribute the Child Goals handout (see appendix 2). Ask them to refer to the form during the discussion. Say that the Child Goals chart will enable them to give accurate feedback to the teacher during the conference following the observation. State that many administrators have used this tool in addition to the Observation Checklist to help them determine which child goals and how many are promoted during each activity. Teachers who have participated in the Spark in-service training will be familiar with the tool.

Distribute Child Goals handout; explain purpose.

Say that if they choose to use this form, they will circle the goals on the chart as they see them promoted during the activity. For example, if a teacher asks questions, administrators will look for goals under either the Language or the Cognition heading. If the children are engaged in art activities, administrators will look for goals under the Fine-Motor, Gross Motor, or Social headings. Help them see that several goals can be promoted while children are doing one thing. For example, if children are playing musical instruments, the goals might include crosses midline, follows two- and three-step verbal commands, rotates wrist to manipulate objects, manipulates objects with motor control, imitates actions of others, moves rhythmically to music, compares attributes (loud/quiet), and shows understanding of positional words. Ask participants to suggest what goals they might be able to mark if they observed a child fingerpainting.

Tell how to use Child Goals form. Give examples.

Say that the form is most effective if they tally the goals and circle the number at the top of the page after the observation. Many of the goals on the chart are ones that are embedded in the activity. If teachers follow the intent of the activity, they will automatically promote many of the goals.

Explain scoring.

Using the Spark Teacher Evaluation Form

Discuss the importance of gaining feedback from the staff. Say that a vitally important piece of information about the impact of the Spark curriculum on the early childhood program can be elicited from the teachers. Suggest that this information can let them know how teachers perceive the curriculum and how they may need to increase their support to teachers. Distribute copies of the Teacher Evaluation form (see appendix 1). They may use the form to solicit this information from staff about their perceptions of ways the curriculum may be improved. Say that this form is most effective when it is used at the end of the year after teachers have gained experience in using the curriculum.

State that the form will provide an opportunity for teachers to express their concerns as well as their satisfaction with the curriculum. Administrators might use this information to help them determine how they can provide assistance to teachers if assistance is needed, for example, by providing additional supplies or extra copies of the story books, if either of these issues arises.

Using the Spark Parent Evaluation Form

Discuss parent communication.

Say that parent feedback about their perceptions of the program is very important, but that sometimes it can be difficult to obtain. Invite discussion as to why it might be difficult and how the problem might be solved. Be sure the discussion includes the following points: Some parents may have trouble communicating through written forms; many are very busy with work and family responsibilities; for some, English is not their first language. One thing is certain, however: All parents are vitally concerned about their children.

Say that parents often need product/process difference explained.

Suggest that the program may have changed dramatically, and that parents may have difficulty accepting the change. Note that the reason most early childhood teachers have the children make craft-like products is because parents expect them. If the teachers in your program have always focused on having the children make products and take them home, the parents will need an explanation of the Spark program early in the year. The explanation can help prevent parent dissatisfaction. Suggest that parents need to know that if they keep the work their child brings home, they will be able to see growth through the year. Their child will often be making a product, but it will not be just like other children's products. They also need to be assured that the work they see will be their child's unique creation.

Distribute copies of the Parent Evaluation form (see appendix 1). This form determines parent satisfaction with the Spark curriculum and provides information to staff about how the curriculum can be improved. It may either be sent home with the child or be used verbally during parent/teacher conferences to initiate a discussion. The second use tends to be more effective, but some parents have difficulty giving negative feedback to the teacher during a conference. The form can be sent home at the end of the year or several times during the year.

Distribute Parent Evaluation form and explain.

Summary

State that by using the four evaluation forms, administrators will obtain a comprehensive impression of how the Spark curriculum is affecting their early childhood programs. They will know how effective the in-service training was by the way the teachers implement the curriculum and by their use of the recommended teaching strategies.

Feedback from the Spark Teacher Evaluation form will also provide information about whether or not the teachers perceive the training as adequate, and it will enable administrators to determine teacher satisfaction with the curriculum. They will be able to determine from the teacher feedback what additional types of support they may need to provide for the teachers and whether or not the teachers may need additional Spark training.

Finally, the Spark Parent Evaluation form will provide information about the impact Spark has made on the child and the response of the family to what is taking place in the classroom.

The composite results of teacher performance, teacher satisfaction, and parent satisfaction will give administrators a comprehensive view of the impact the Spark curriculum has made on their programs.

APPENDIX 1:

Checklists and Evaluation Forms

Spark Observation Checklist
Cover Sheet

Observer:_____   Date:_____

Teacher:_____   Unit:_____

A.M. Class_____   P.M. Class _____

School/Program:_____

- -

Spark Observation Checklist
Cover Sheet

Observer:_____   Date:_____

Teacher:_____   Unit:_____

A.M. Class_____   P.M. Class _____

School/Program:_____

Large-Group (Storytelling) Activity Observation Checklist

Teacher/Aide_____ Duration of Activity_____

	Yes	No
1. Materials were gathered before activity started.	O	O
2. Previous day's story was reviewed.	O	O
3. Previous day's center activities were reviewed.	O	O

4. The story was presented:
a. The teacher read the story in an enthusiastic manner,
   e.g., used voice inflections. .... O O
b. Children were encouraged to participate by
   • chanting repeated story lines .... O O
   • performing physical actions .... O O
   • other .... O O
c. The story was discussed. .... O O

5. Throughout the activity:
a. The teacher asked questions that were
   • closed*   o (1–3)   o (4–5)   o (6+) .... O O
   • open*   o (1–3)   o (4–5)   o (6+) .... O O
b. The teacher encouraged children to share experiences. ...... O O
c. The teacher gave children positive feedback that was
   • non-specific* o (1–3) o (4–5) o (6+) .... O O
   • specific*   o (1–3) o (4–5) o (6+) .... O O

6. The concept/theme of the day was introduced as suggested:
a. The teacher demonstrated* the concept/theme. .... O O
b. The teacher discussed the concept/theme. .... O O
c. Child(ren) participated in demonstration of concept/theme. ...... O O

7. Center activities were introduced:
a. The teacher/aide demonstrated* center activities. .... O O
   o Art   o Make-Believe   o Music
b. The teacher/aide made the center activities enticing.*
   o Art   o Make-Believe   o Music

8. The children chose* their first center of attendance. .... O O

*See Definitions.

Small-Group (Center) Activity Observation Checklist

○ Art   ○ Make-Believe   ○ Music

Teacher/Aide_____   Duration of Activity_____

	Yes	No
1. All suggested materials were gathered before the activity began.	○	○
2. The way in which the activity was implemented enabled children to make choices:*		
a. Choice of materials	○	○
b. Choice of their response to the materials	○	○
3. The fidelity* of the activity was maintained.	○	○
4. The teacher/aide related the activity to the		
a. Story	○	○
b. Concept/Theme of the day	○	○
5. The teacher/aide promoted child growth:		
a. General goals ○(1–9) ○(10+)	○	○
b. Individual objectives ○(1–3) ○(4–5) ○(6+) ○(NA)	○	○
6. The teacher/aide participated* in the activity:		
a. Modeled* behavior	○	○
b. Supported* child growth	○	○
7. The teacher/aide asked questions to stimulate thinking:		
a. Closed* questions ○(1–3) ○(4–5) ○(6+)	○	○
b. Open* questions ○(1–3) ○(4–5) ○(6+)	○	○
8. The teacher/aide gave the children positive meaningful feedback:*		
a. Non-specific* ○(1–3) ○(4–5) ○(6+)	○	○
b. Specific* ○(1–3) ○(4–5) ○(6+)	○	○

*See Definitions.

Definitions for Observation Checklists

Choice: The opportunity to decide which center to attend, what materials to use, and how to use the materials.

Demonstrates: The teacher shows the children what they will be doing at the center. The intent is to enable the children to participate fully in the activity and to provide information that will enable them to make an informed choice of activity, materials, and/or their response to the materials.

Enticing: A way of making the introduction to an activity highly interesting by voice inflection, the use of props, and the general enthusiasm displayed toward the activity.

Fidelity: Retain the original intent of the activity. For example, the activity will have a specific format and suggested procedures. Activities may be modified to fit the needs of the children; however, the concept of the day and general structure of the activity should be maintained.

Models: The adult is actively engaged in the activity: he paints, builds a structure, sings, moves to recorded music, or pretends in the make-believe center. He is primarily one of the group.

Supports: The adult's behavior encourages continued participation by the student in the activity. This category includes talk related to the center activity such as questioning, instructing, and interactive discussion. The instructive talk may be in the form of a song. The intent is to promote child growth.

Positive and meaningful feedback: The adult acknowledges the child's efforts. The feedback is more than affirmation. It may be non-specific ("Good job!" "Good!" "I like that!") or specific ("I like your answer! You're a good thinker!", "Your picture is beautiful. I like the curved lines!" "What an interesting sound you are making!" "Good quiet sound, Juan!") The category of specific feedback also includes feedback related to child behavior during the activity ("Good listening, Joshua!" "I like the way you are sitting, Malika.")

Questions: Questions related to the activity or story. This category does not include maintenance questions such as "Did you wash your hands?"

> **Closed:** A question to which the teacher is seeking a specific answer, such as "What shape is this?" or "What is the name of the book?"

> **Open:** A question for which there is no one correct answer; the teacher is asking for the child's opinion or for the child to share an experience: "Which one of your pictures do you like the best?" "What do you do before you go to bed at night?"

Spark Teacher Evaluation Form

It's The End of the Year—How Did Spark Go?

We are eager to know how the Spark program affected you and the children you work with. Please let us know what worked for you and if there were any special challenges in implementing Spark. We think this questionnaire will take 10–15 minutes of your time, but it will be invaluable to us. Thanks for all your hard work!

1. How did children react to the stories?

Stories represented events or ideas that were familiar to children.
O most children   O some children   O a few children

Stories helped children learn about different cultures or lifestyles.
O most stories   O some stories   O a few stories

The children learned to join in the stories with words or movements.
O usually   O sometimes   O not very often

The children remained interested in the stories even after hearing them several times.
O most children   O some children   O a few children

What else should we know about the stories?

_____

_____

2. How did children react to the art, music, and make-believe activities?

Children were eager to choose centers.
O usually   O sometimes   O not very often

Children stayed at a center for 5–10 minutes.
O usually   O sometimes   O not very often

Children used Spark songs or music in other contexts, after the activities were over.
O usually   O sometimes   O not very often

Anything else we should know about the arts activities?

_____

_____

3. How easy was it to integrate the Spark curriculum into your teaching?

It affected my planning and preparation time.
O **took less time**   O **about the same**   O **took more time**

It affected the way I arrange my classroom.
O **not at all**   O **somewhat**   O **quite a bit**

It affected the way I organized my time and routines.
O **not at all**   O **somewhat**   O **quite a bit**

What else should we know about organizing for Spark?

_____

_____

4. How did Spark affect your teaching strategies?

I asked more questions.
O **during stories**   O **during centers**   O **not much**

I talked to the children more about ideas and concepts.
O **during stories**   O **during centers**   O **not much**

The Spark training prepared me to implement Spark.
O **very much**   O **somewhat**   O **not enough**

I thought more about which individual objectives might be met during activities.
O **during stories**   O **during centers**   O **not much**

I adapted the Spark model to fit my classroom and my teaching.
O **quite a bit**   O **somewhat**   O **not at all**

What else should we know about Spark and your teaching strategies?

_____

_____

Was there anything that was particularly helpful or difficult about implementing Spark (for example: training, curriculum materials, format, support from administrator or colleagues, parent involvement)?

_____

_____

Spark Parent Evaluation

We would like to know what you think about the Spark program that has been used in your child's class this year.

1. Did your child seem to enjoy the Spark program? How could you tell?

_____

_____

_____

_____

2. Did you read any of the Spark books at home with your child? Which books?

_____

_____

_____

_____

3. Did your child talk about the Spark stories or activities at home? Which stories did your child seem to like the best?

_____

_____

_____

_____

4. What kinds of activities did your child talk about? Singing, dancing, doing art, or pretending in make-believe?

_____

_____

_____

_____

Thanks for your help!

APPENDIX 2:

Child Goals

Child Goals

Teacher Name _____ Unit/Activity _____ Date _____

Cognitive	Language	Fine Motor	Gross Motor	Social
○ Shows understanding of opposites (hot/cold, slow/fast)	○ Shows understanding of positional words	○ Rotates wrist to manipulate objects	○ Runs smoothly and changes direction	○ Follows simple rules with reminder/without reminder
○ Shows understanding of size relationships (big/little, long/short)	○ Responds to adverbs, (loudly, quietly)	○ Holds paper with one hand, draws or writes with other hand	○ Walks sideways, walks forward, walks backward, walks on tiptoes	○ Follows simple rules in game
○ Compares attributes (soft/hard, loud/quiet, heavy/light)	○ Identifies quiet and loud sounds	○ Folds sheet of paper	○ Walks along a narrow path	○ Asserts self in socially acceptable ways
○ Sorts objects by two or more attributes	○ Answers yes or no appropriately	○ Crumples piece of paper	○ Hops on one foot	○ Attends to teacher-directed task for 10–15 minutes
○ Answers simple questions	○ Responds to who, what, where, and when questions	○ Uses two hands in opposing movement	○ Jumps forward, jumps backward, jumps over object, jumps in place	○ Participates in group activities
○ Engages in problem solving	○ Answers questions about story	○ Cuts with scissors	○ Throws/catches object	○ Waits turn for teacher attention
○ Recalls words to song	○ Recalls events from story	○ Paints dots and circles	○ Gallops/skips	○ Asks for adult help when needed
○ Recalls facts from story	○ Participates in songs or chants	○ Imitates vertical line, circle, cross, shapes, letters, simple words, numerals	○ Rolls objects/self	○ Takes turns
○ Identifies textures	○ Contributes to group discussion	○ Copies vertical lines, circles, cross, shapes, letters, simple words, numerals	○ Twirls around	○ Interacts appropriately with other children
○ ID/labels body parts	○ Acts out familiar story	○ Traces shapes and lines	○ Imitates actions of others	○ Shares
○ Matches, points to, labels colors	○ Imitates characters from story	○ Draws lines, cross, shapes independently	○ Moves rhythmically to music	
			○ Crawls/creeps	

continued . . .

Child Goals (Continued)

Cognitive	Language	Fine Motor	Gross Motor	Social
o Matches, points to, labels shapes	o Participates in movements related to story	o Uses paste or glue		o Experiments appropriately with classroom materials
o ID/labels past and present activities	o Relates own experiences	o Crosses midline		o Asks permission to use others' possessions
o Labels familiar objects	o Labels own creations	o Uses dynamic pencil grasp		o Finishes projects
o Labels members of a category	o Uses names of others	o Rolls clay into balls and ropes		o Plans and builds constructively
o ID and labels same/ different	o Follows two- and three-step verbal commands	o Strings beads		o Leads others during activities
o Recognizes, prints, spells first name	o Labels/describes items/objects	o Stacks objects		o Initiates peer contact
o Counts by rote, meaningful counting	o Shows understanding of simple quantity concepts (one, some, all, many)	o Prints letters		o Uses imagination in play
o Divides whole into halves	o Engages in short dialogue with peers	o Claps hands		o Labels facial expression of primary emotions
o Carries out multistep activity		o Manipulates objects with motor control		o Verbalizes own feelings
o Makes suggestions		o Uses left-to-right progression		o Says please and thank you appropriately
o Shows awareness of outcomes		o Imitates hand motions		

APPENDIX 3:

References

References

Adams, M. J. 1990. *Beginning to read: Thinking and learning about print.* Cambridge, Massachusetts: MIT Press.

Alper, C. D. 1992. Early childhood music education. In *The early childhood curriculum: A review of current research,* ed. C. Seefeldt. New York: Teachers College Press.

Atwater, J. B., J. J. Carta, I. A. Schwartz, and S. R. McConnell. 1994. Blending developmentally appropriate practice and early childhood special education. In *Diversity and developmentally appropriate practice,* ed. B. L. Mallory and R. S. New, 185–201. New York: Teachers College Press.

Barrera, I. 1993. Effective and appropriate instruction for all children: The challenge of cultural/linguistic diversity and young children with special needs. *Topics in Early Childhood Special Education,* 13:461–87.

Beaty, J. 1997. *Building bridges with multi-cultural picture books.* Upper Saddle River, New Jersey: Prentice-Hall.

Berk, L. E. 1994. Vygotsky's theory: The importance of make-believe play. *Young Children,* November 1994:30–39.

Derman-Sparks, L., and C. B. Brunson-Phillips. 1997. *Teaching/learning anti-racism: A developmental approach.* New York: Teachers College Press.

Dickinson, D. K., and M. W. Smith. 1994. Long-term effects of preschool teachers' book readings on low-income children's vocabulary and story comprehension. *Reading Research Quarterly* 29 (2):105–22.

Dunst, C., G. Mahoney, and K. Buchan. 1996. Promoting the cognitive competence of young children with or at risk for developmental disabilities. In *Early intervention/ early childhood special education: Recommended practices,* S. Odom and M. McLean, eds. Austin, Texas: Pro-ed.

Fox, L., M. Hanline, C. Vail, and K. Galant. 1994. Developmentally appropriate practice: Applications for young children with disabilities. *Journal of Early Intervention* 18 (3):243–57.

Garcia, E., and B. McLaughlin, eds. 1995. Meeting the challenge of linguistic and cultural diversity in early childhood education. New York: Teachers College Press.

Gonzalez-Mena, J. 1997. *Multi-cultural issues in child care.* 2d ed. Mountain View, California: Mayfield.

Hauser-Cram, P., and M. Kraus. 1991. Measuring change in children and families. *Journal of Early Intervention* 15:288–97.

Heath, S.B., and L. Mangiola, L. 1991. *Children of promise: Literate activities in linguistically and culturally diverse classrooms.* (A joint publication of National Education Association, Center for the Study of Writing and Literacy, and American Educational Research Association). Washington, D.C.: National Education Association.

Hohmann, M., and D. Weikart. 1995. *Educating young children: Active practices for preschool and child care programs.* Ypsilanti, Michigan: High Scope Press.

International Reading Association and National Association for the Education of Young Children. 1998. Learning to read and write: Developmentally appropriate practices for young children. (Joint position statement.) *Young Children* 53:30–46.

Jalongo, M.R. 1988. *Young children and picture books: Literature from infancy to six.* Washington, D.C.: National Association for the Education of Young Children.

Lewman, B. 1999. Read it again! *Children and Families* 18 (1) (Winter 1999):12–15.

Lynch, E., and M. Hanson. 1998. *Developing cross-cultural competence: A guide for working with young children and their families.* 2d ed. Baltimore: Paul H. Brookes.

McWilliam, R. A., and D. B. Bailey. 1992. Promoting engagement and mastery. In *Teaching infants and preschoolers with disabilities,* D. B. Bailey and M. Wolery, eds. 2d ed. 229–55. New York: Merrill.

National Academy of Sciences: Committee on the Prevention of Reading Difficulties in Young Children. 1998. *Preventing reading difficulties in young children.* Washington, D.C.: National Academy Press.

Rab, V., and K. Wood. 1995. *Child care and the ADA: A handbook for inclusive programs.* Baltimore: Paul H. Brookes.

Scott, C. R. 1989. How children grow—musically. *Music Education* 76 (2):28–31.

Smith, R.B. 1970. *Music in the child's education.* New York: Ronald Press.

Snow, C.E., M.S. Burns, and P. Griffin, eds. 1998. Preschool-specific recommendations for state leadership. Excerpts from *Preventing reading difficulties in young children.* National Research Council. (1998). Washington, D.C.: National Academy Press.

Snow, C., and B. Goldfield. 1993. Turn the page, please: Situation-specific language acquisition. *Journal of Child Language* 10:551–69.

The state of America's children: Yearbook 1998. Washington, D.C.: Children's Defense Fund.

Teaching Tolerance Project. 1997. *Starting small: Teaching tolerance in preschool and early grades.* Montgomery, Alabama: Southern Poverty Law Center.

Whitehurst, G., and C. Lonigan. 1998. Child development and emergent literacy. *Child Development* 69:848–72.

Wolery, M., and D. Sainato. 1996. General curriculum and intervention strategies. In *Early intervention and early childhood special education: Recommended practices,* S. Odom and M. McLean, eds. Austin, Texas: Pro-ed.

Yaden, D. 1988. Understanding stories through repeated read-alouds: How many does it take? *The Reading Teacher* 41(6):556–61.

York, S. 1991. *Roots and wings: Affirming culture in early childhood programs.* St. Paul: Redleaf Press.

Index

Reproducible overhead pages, which do not have page numbers, are designated in the index by overhead (OH) number, followed by page number in parentheses: OH204(p.132).